# UNEMPLOYMENT, MONEY WAGE RATES, AND INFLATION

# M.I.T. MONOGRAPHS IN ECONOMICS

# UNEMPLOYMENT, MONEY WAGE RATES, AND INFLATION

GEORGE L. PERRY

## THE M.I.T. PRESS

*Massachusetts Institute of Technology*
*Cambridge, Massachusetts, and London, England*

*TO MY FATHER AND MOTHER*

# Preface

The present volume represents a minor extension of a doctoral thesis submitted at the Massachusetts Institute of Technology in August 1961. Final preparation of the thesis for publication was postponed while I served on the staff of the Council of Economic Advisers from 1961 to 1963. It then seemed appropriate to add the material now appearing in Chapter 4, which examines developments in the first three years after the original regressions were run. This material and most of Chapter 6 on the implications of the results for economic policy are the main additions to the original thesis.

Some cutoff point had to be selected if such a study were ever to reach the publishers, and wage developments in 1964 and 1965 were not tested formally against predictions from the equations. However, I should take this opportunity to report that recent wage increases have been more modest than one could have predicted from past experience with any of the equations estimated here, or almost certainly, with any equation of this general type. While it is somehow pleasing to see one's empirical research validated indefinitely by subsequent observations, the favorable twist that these recent observations suggest for the unemployment-inflation choice that confronts us more than compensates for my technician's chagrin. In any case, even when their forecasts go astray, estimated equations are valuable precisely because they signal us when new developments require explanation. It is hard to say whether the government's active concern over wage and price decisions is largely, or even partly, reponsible for the recent wage moderation. But some explanation is in order, and this is at least a plausible hypothesis.

In the period since 1961, a considerable amount of new work has been done on this general subject. In my judgment, this more recent work has been sufficiently different in the questions it has asked and answered that it has not been necessary to revise the material in this thesis. These recent writings have been included in the bibliography to this volume. I should call attention especially to the two works listed there by Eckstein and Wilson and by Eckstein which specifically introduce the profit variable in explaining wages in the United States.

Some of the results of the thesis were presented in a paper read at the Econometric Society Meetings in December 1962. Much of the material in the present Chapters 3 and 4 appeared in "The Determinants of Wage Rate Changes and the Inflation-Unemployment Trade-off for the United States," in *The Review of Economic Studies,* October 1964, and appears here with the permission of its editor.

I am grateful for fellowship support from the United States Steel Foundation and from the Ford Foundation received during the time the thesis was written, and for research assistance provided from the University of Minnesota's graduate school research funds during the preparation of this volume. The facilities of the M.I.T. Computation Center were used in doing the statistical work in the study.

My main and major debt is to Robert Solow. His suggestion originally got me interested in this subject. He far exceeded the formal duties of thesis adviser in offering helpful comments, useful ideas, and needed encouragement, despite being on leave from M.I.T. during the period when most of this work was being done. And he has subsequently read and commented on the drafts of the new material in the present volume. I am also grateful to several others for their help at various stages of this work. Carlos Díaz and Norman Simler read an earlier draft of the present volume and offered extensive comments and criticisms that have improved its content and form. Albert Ando, Franklin Fisher, Edward Foster, and Edwin Kuh helped with problems and questions that arose in connection with the original thesis and offered suggestions that have aided in the preparation of the present volume.

My wife Jean continually provided cheerful support, for which I am especially grateful, and helped with typing and proofreading. G. Brent Davidson, Lillian Dayos, Julian Greene, and Daina Smits all helped with calculations, data processing, drafting and other details. And Cheryl Skillman skillfully typed the final manuscript.

GEORGE L. PERRY

*Minneapolis, Minnesota*
*August 1965*

# Contents

# List of Tables

# List of Figures

# List of Principal Symbols Used

Variables designated by lower-case letters are percentage changes. Variables designated by upper-case letters are levels. The lack of a subscript indicates a variable is dated in the present quarter. More extensive definitions and explanations are given in the text and the Appendix.

$W$   rate of straight-time hourly earnings.

$w$   percentage change in $W$ over the past year (four quarters)

$C$   consumer price index

$c$   percentage change in $C$ over the past year

$U$   average unemployment rate during the past year

$R$   average rate of return on stockholders' equity over the past year

$\Delta R$   quarterly first difference in $R$

$^m p$   annual percentage change in manufacturing output prices

$^s p$   annual percentage change in the price of services to consumers

$^f p$   annual percentage change in raw food prices

$^r p$   annual percentage change in the index of raw material prices

$(Q/K)$   index of average manufacturing capacity utilization during the past year

$\Delta(Q/K)$   quarterly first difference in the $(Q/K)$ index

# 1

# Introduction and Review
# of Recent Studies

## Introduction

With the Great Depression of the 1930's over and Keynesian income
analysis firmly rooted as an explanation of underemployment equilibrium, economists since the war have turned their attention increasingly to the problem of inflation. The demand-pull explanation,
as exemplified either by the neoclassical quantity theory or the
Keynesian aggregate excess-demand model, has yielded equal prominence to a class of cost-push explanations and to others based on
the disaggregated behavior of the economy and on assymetries between the upward and downward movement of wages and prices.

The history of postwar price behavior has provided evidence for
more than one view. The strongest burst of inflation occurred immediately after the end of the war. By September 1948, the Consumer
Price Index had risen 35.2 percent from its level at war's end, and
the Wholesale Price Index had risen 54.4 percent. This period is
now generally acknowledged as one characterized by excess aggregate demand. During the war, households and firms had accumu-
lated large supplies of liquid assets. Private debt had been greatly
reduced. The stock of both consumers' and producers' durable goods
had been depleted both by the war and the depression years that
preceded it. In this environment of acute needs and abundant purchasing power, the effective demand of the private sector far exceeded the capacity of the economy to produce the goods demanded
even with the drastic reduction of government expenditures that
occurred. The results were high profit rates and rising prices and
wages. Although the interrelations among these three elements are
subjects for study, in part the aim of this book, the aggregate excess

1

demand that existed is widely acknowledged as the primary factor behind all the manifestations of inflation observed for the period.

The next episode of inflation came with the onset of Korean hostilities and was again broadly a product of excess aggregate demand, fueled by the desires of consumers and businesses to build up stocks of goods. These demands by consumers for automobiles and other durable goods and by businesses for additional inventories were superimposed upon a boom year in residential construction and the beginning of the step-up in military expenditures. As a result, in the eight months starting June 1950, consumer prices rose by 8.0 percent and wholesale prices by 16.3 percent.

The last spell of general inflation occurred over the three years beginning in mid-1955. During this time, consumer prices rose by 8.0 percent and wholesale prices by 8.9 percent. In contrast to the two earlier periods of price rise, excess demand in the classic sense was present during very little of this period, if at all. This is not to say that demand was not relatively strong; but there was little sign of actual shortages at prevailing prices to explain the inflation. Profit rates were high, wages rose at relatively fast rates, and prices in most sectors climbed gradually. Unemployment rates hovered near 4 percent.

It is this last period that inspired much of the recent discussion of inflation and gave such prominence to cost-push explanations and other treatments outside the realm of general excess-demand theories. The most careful analysis of price behavior in the period is that of Charles L. Schultze[1] in his Joint Economic Committee monograph.

Throughout the whole postwar period, wages were behaving in a manner roughly parallel to prices, generally rising fastest during the inflationary periods. This roughly similar behavior, quite natural as it is, has led to the characterization of the wage-price question as the standard chicken-and-egg problem of economics. Perhaps in part because of this, until recently little work had been done on providing empirical information about the behavior of wage rates under varying economic conditions. This has been true despite the fact that within the framework of most theories, discussions of inflation point to the behavior of wages as a key to understanding price movements. In some views, wage increases are the initiating force in inflation and must play the primary role in an explanation. In

[1] Schultze, Charles L., Study Paper No. 1, "Recent Inflation in the United States," Joint Economic Committee, Washington, D.C. (September 1959).

others, wages play a more passive role, but at a minimum must pursue price increases in order to maintain sufficient demand to validate the price rises. The problems associated with establishing causality in these questions are formidable, and indeed a simple answer appropriate to all circumstances is probably not available. In an economy as far from the competitive ideal as that of any modern nation, there is ample scope for some wage increases to force up prices as well as for administered price increases to lead to large wage demands, not to mention the complex of intermediate patterns that has been described and discussed.

Nevertheless, despite the lack of agreement on a detailed theory explaining aggregate price and output movements, a fairly general consensus exists among economists for describing what broad relationships to expect. At some level of unemployment, considerably above what most economists understand as full employment, prices start rising. Successively higher levels of activity are associated, roughly at least, with correspondingly larger rates of price increase. In this situation, the more traditional problem of adjusting aggregate demand so as to reach full employment without overshooting into the area of inflation must be replaced by the dual problems of deciding what combination of unemployment and inflation to aim at and then adjusting aggregate demand to reach this point.

In keeping with this description of events, and in recognition of the link between labor costs and prices, the empirical questions to which several writers have addressed themselves recently are whether a predictable relationship exists between unemployment and wage changes and what the relationship looks like.

The first work that made a substantial contribution in this direction was an article published in 1958 by A. W. Phillips.[2] This study will be discussed further, but its general hypothesis deserves mention in this introductory section as well. Phillips tested for a relation between aggregate unemployment and aggregate money wage rates. His results indicated that there is a relation between these variables such that the lower the unemployment level, the faster the rate of wage increase. This Phillips curve, as the relation has come to be known, gave substance to much of the prevailing opinion about a modern free economy's inflationary behavior. It emphasized the view that policymakers must choose between varying combinations

[2] Phillips, A. W., "The Relation Between Unemployment and the Rate of Change of Money Wage Rates in the United Kingdom, 1861–1957," *Economica*, N.S. 25 (November 1958).

of rates of wage increase (and hence inflation) and levels of unemployment.

The present study proceeds in a somewhat different spirit from
Phillips'. The relation between rates of wage change and unemployment levels is still a point of major interest; but the present study
replaces the Phillips curve notion with a locus of points taken from
a *family* of curves. Each of these curves represents a *ceteris paribus*
relation between rates of wage change and unemployment levels, in
contrast to the *mutatis mutandis* relation of the Phillips curve.[3]

The contrasting implications for policy of these two views are
important. Rather than restricting choices to a single Phillips curve
with its rigid trade-off between unemployment and inflation, the
family-of-curves theory points out a wider range of choices available
for intelligent policymaking. By recognizing the possibility of
moving to different wage change-unemployment curves, it shows
that one can improve the terms on which the inflation-unemployment choice is made.

Translating the discussion into the terms of statistical analysis,
the present study uses multiple regression techniques to estimate
the effect on aggregate wage rates of *several* key variables that
influence wage determination in the economy. Unemployment is
one of these, and the unemployment-wage change relation that is
estimated from this analysis shows what happens to wages for different levels of unemployment when the other variables take on
some fixed values. As the values of some or all of these other variables change, the wage-unemployment relation shifts.

In examining the behavior of aggregate wages in this way, an
essentially agnostic position is taken with regard to the different
theories of inflation. The course of wages is described by the estimated relation, and wage changes can be traced to the explanatory
variables. It is the relation between wage changes and these explanatory variables that is important. Our interest will be in the
nature of these relationships and in whether they are constant or
changing. The results may provide information that supports a particular explanation of inflation for some period; but the formulation

[3] Instead of assuming that a Phillips curve treatment deliberately depicts the
relation when other things change as they will, one might argue it is a *ceteris
paribus* relation based on a theory that nothing else matters (or that anything
else that is relevant to explaining wage changes is perfectly correlated with unemployment). But these are matters for investigation, not assertion. And to the
degree they are found untrue, the Phillips curve is in fact a *mutatis mutandis*
relation.

of the problem in this way does not depend on any theory of inflation nor does it commit us to a sharp distinction between competing
theories. The notion of inflationary or noninflationary rates of wage
change is developed with neutral assumptions about the relative
share of wage income, the composition of output, and other potentially complicating factors.

In addition to its intensive investigation of the wage relation for
the postwar years, this study compares the results for that period
with those of an earlier time to see if basic changes have occurred
in the economy which might make it more prone to inflation than
before. The postwar years themselves are then divided into two
periods to examine the stability of the wage relation over that
interval. Finally, equations explaining prices and profits are estimated for the postwar years, and the interrelationship between them
and the wage equation is examined to see what light they shed on
the inflationary process. Expanding the analysis to include several
equations also allows us to employ an approximation to a consistent estimating technique and to examine the possibility of bias
arising in estimating the wage equation alone.

Before presenting the model tested in this study, it will be of
interest to review some of the recent work by other authors who
have made empirical studies of aggregate wage behavior.

## A Survey of Recent Work: The British Case

### A. W. Phillips

The forerunner of recent attempts to analyze aggregate wage
behavior is the aforementioned study by A. W. Phillips[4] on the
relationship between wage changes and unemployment. Dealing
with the United Kingdom, he tests the hypothesis that the percentage rate of change of money wage rates can be explained largely
by the percentage unemployment in the labor force and the rate of
change of this unemployment. The data he uses to test this proposition cover most of the period from 1861 to 1957. Not only does
Phillips conclude that the hypothesis is correct, but perhaps most
interesting, he claims that the form of the relationship between the
rate of change of money wage rates and the unemployment variables is quite stable over the whole period studied. This last conclusion suggests that the institutional characteristics of the wage-de-

---

[4] Phillips, A. W., *op. cit.*

termining process, which have changed so completely over the course of Phillips' time period, are of little significance compared with the fundamental economic variables affecting wage rates.

The other main assertion made by Phillips is that the relation between wage changes and unemployment is highly nonlinear. As he puts it:

> When the demand for labor is high and there are very few unemployed we should expect employers to bid wage rates up quite rapidly, each firm and each industry being continually tempted to offer a little above the prevailing rates to attract the most suitable labor from other firms and industries. On the other hand, it appears that workers are reluctant to offer their services at less than the prevailing rates when the demand for labor is low and unemployment is high so that wage rates fall only very slowly. The relation between unemployment and the rate of change of wage rates is therefore likely to be highly non-linear.[5]

In order to accommodate this assertion in his hypothesis, Phillips uses a logarithmic form $(1/W)(dW/dt) = a + bU^c$ for testing the relationship between wage change and unemployment. This form is an unfortunate choice. Since wages sometimes fall in the period studied, negative logarithms would be necessary to express some of the data points. Phillips avoids this problem by grouping all observations according to unemployment levels and then averaging the wage changes for each group. With the number of points thus compressed, he fits the relation by trial and error. A different form for the relation would have allowed more direct methods of fitting to be used and facilitated much further experimentation. Such a change is made in a subsequent paper discussed later in this chapter.

Equipped with a regression curve relating wage changes and unemployment, Phillips then observes the effect of the rate of change of unemployment from looking at the time path of the scatter diagram between the first two variables. He notes that this time path takes the form of loops around the regression curve for most subperiods studied. When unemployment is falling, the points lie above the curve, indicating wages rising faster than average; and when unemployment is rising, the points lie below the curve, showing wages rising more slowly than the expected rate for each level of unemployment.

The conclusions, admittedly tentative, which Phillips reaches

[5] *Ibid.*, p. 283.

about the effect of unemployment are interesting. Besides apparently supporting the general hypotheses just described, he interprets his results to indicate that in the absence of rapid increases in import prices and with productivity increases of 2 percent per year, the price level would remain stable with an unemployment rate of $2\frac{1}{2}$ percent.[6, 7]

Phillips assigns a distinctly secondary role to prices in the wage-determining process. Percentage increases in the cost of living, when they are extreme, are used to explain large deviations of wage changes from those predicted by unemployment. In discussing the post-World War II period, he elaborates on this treatment and uses it to characterize different years as periods governed by a demand-pull or cost-push environment.

For this period, and implicitly for earlier periods although they receive shorter attention, Phillips identifies changes in the cost of living arising from exogenous factors, such as changing import prices as cost effects. His hypothesis on the role of unemployment in affecting wages treats unemployment as a measure of the strength of the demand for labor. Rather than use the two effects as simultaneously determining wages, he postulates a process whereby the demand forces generate whatever wage increase was not already forthcoming from cost-of-living considerations. So long as the cost of living does not rise so fast as to exceed the wage increase which would be forthcoming from the pure demand effect as reflected in unemployment, the cost effect is inoperative. In years when the cost of living does rise faster than the rise in wages predicted by unemployment alone, the cost effects dominate and the resultant wage increase is larger than predicted by unemployment.

From the present study's view of the problem, the central drawback to Phillips' study is his inattention to other variables that may have significant independent effects on the rate of wage changes. The minor role that he forces onto living costs and the complete omission of other potential variables, particularly a measure of profitability, make his formulation too restrictive.

[6] *Ibid.*, p. 299.

[7] It should be pointed out here that the British figures for unemployment are not directly comparable with those for the United States. The British figures are taken from registrations for unemployment compensation, while in this country they are obtained by sample surveys. There is some evidence, cited in Chapter 3, that the British figure should be increased by half for comparison with the United States.

*Richard G. Lipsey*

Following Phillips' study, several other writers reported empirical work on the question of wage determination, some prompted directly by his study and others reporting parallel investigations. Richard G. Lipsey's paper[8] is the closest to Phillips', being in fact a careful reconsideration of it. His analysis provides at least two substantial improvements over the original. By choosing analytically more useful forms for the relation tested, he is able to look precisely at many questions that Phillips left as interesting speculations. And by formulating a rather careful theory about the relation between wages and unemployment, he can offer consistent explanations for many of the observed results. As it turns out, Phillips' main results are supported and buttressed considerably, while some secondary observations are rejected. However, although Lipsey brings in price changes more openly, his formulation still excludes other variables and requires the same reservations expressed with respect to Phillips' study in this regard.

Lipsey uses the forms $(1/W)(dW/dt) = a + bU^{-1} + cU^{-2}$ and $(1/W)(dW/dt) = a + bU^{-1} + cU^{-4}$ to measure the relation between wage changes and unemployment. The first is used to explain the years up through 1913. The second, which displays much sharper curvature, is used for the later years, up to 1957. To these two forms, Lipsey subsequently adds $(1/U)(dU/dt)$ and $(1/P)$ $(dP/dt)$, measures of the rate of change of unemployment and prices, to test their effect as further explanatory variables.

The model used is seemingly not too different from Phillips', but it is developed with greater care and has one important difference which Lipsey explores fully. Unemployment is considered a measure of excess demand in the labor market by both writers, although Lipsey develops the connection between the two concepts more carefully. But his main departure comes in applying the structural theory of this excess demand interpretation on a disaggregated basis. His theory asserts a connection between the rate of wage change and unemployment in different sectors of the economy. Because of the nonlinear nature of this relation, differences in unemployment between the various sectors will result in observations on the aggregate variables for the whole economy lying above the true

[8] Lipsey, Richard G., "The Relation Between Unemployment and the Rate of Change of Money Wage Rates in the United Kingdom, 1862–1957: A Further Analysis," *Economica*, N.S. 27 (February 1960).

structural relation for the individual sectors. In short, the observed aggregate percentage wage changes for various aggregate levels of unemployment will be greater than the percentage wage changes for individual sectors which would be associated with the unemployment level of those sectors. The more uneven the distribution of unemployment between sectors, the more the aggregate observations will differ from the structural microrelations.

This last observation leads Lipsey to an interesting argument. He uses it to explain Phillips' observed relation of wage changes to the rate of change of unemployment. If, over the course of a cycle, there is a systematic variation in the inequality of unemployment among different sectors of the economy, there should result a systematic variation in the degree of displacement of the observed aggregate data from the structural microrelations. This would be so if, on the upswing of a cycle, the growth in demand is typically uneven between sectors, while on the downswing it is relatively even with unemployment rising together in all sectors.

While Lipsey makes highly resourceful and interesting use of his data, several of his secondary conclusions are subject to question. He divides Phillips' long period in two, examining the pre- and post-World War I years separately. The role of unemployment and price changes in explaining wage changes seems well established in both periods, although, as he points out, the relative importance of prices appears to be greater in the latter period. However, the effect he measures for the rate of change of unemployment seems doubtful, possibly because of the inaccuracy of annual data for such a variable. Its coefficient changes from negative to positive in the latter period, which is grounds for dismissing it as a legitimate behavioral variable. Also, Lipsey's aggregation explanation itself seems questionable. It depends on a considerable nonlinearity in the wage change-unemployment relation, and on the existence of reasonably isolated labor market sectors with wages in each responding to unemployment in each and with the unemployment among different sectors being sufficiently uncorrelated. The sort of explanation given by Lipsey fails if any of these three conditions is not met. Whether they are met is basically an empirical question, although one may doubt that they are on *a priori* grounds. Regarding the first condition, Lipsey's own paper offers some evidence that it is not met.[9] Although over the whole period studied there occurs a wide range

[9] *Ibid.*, footnote 2, p. 27.

of unemployment, this is not true over smaller subperiods such as those that would give rise, in the model used, to the cyclical loops caused by aggregation.

Both Phillips' and Lipsey's studies suffer from the limitations of annual data. Their choice was necessary since they examined long historical periods over which more detailed data are not available. But it is doubtful that their annual figures can reveal more than the most basic relationships. As was just mentioned, rate-of-change variables probably require more delicate treatment than is possible with annual data, and short lags between the relevant variables cannot be accounted for.

### L. A. Dicks-Mireaux and J. C. R. Dow

Another significant study of this problem that avoids the inaccuracies of annual data was made recently by L. A. Dicks-Mireaux and J. C. R. Dow.[10] They concentrate on the post-World War II period in Britain, doing an extensive analysis of the years from 1946 to 1956. By focusing on these recent years, they are able to use quarterly variables rather than annual ones and to consider some broad industry groups separately in addition to doing an aggregated study.

The hypothesis tested by Dicks-Mireaux and Dow is that the rate of wage change is a function both of the pressure of demand and the rate of price change. Thus they take account of the role of prices more openly than the authors previously mentioned. Their reason is a suspicion that the connection between wages and prices has become stronger since the war and would mask the relation of unemployment to wages if not taken into account. In this, they share the opinion of Lipsey, although the lack of a strong connection between wages and prices in the prewar years has not been demonstrated convincingly by either.

The demand for labor is a variable based on statistics of unemployment and unfilled vacancies as developed in an earlier paper.[11] The index follows closely the inverse of percentage unemployment, and the authors get similar results when actually using unemployment as an explanatory variable. The demand-for-labor variable will

---

[10] Dicks-Mireaux, L. A., and J. C. R. Dow, "The Determinants of Wage Inflation: The United Kingdom, 1946–1956," *The Journal of the Royal Statistical Society,* Series A, 22(2) (1959).

[11] Dow, J. C. R., and L. A. Dicks-Mireaux, "Excess Demand for Labor," *Oxford Economic Papers,* N.S. 10 (February 1959).

be referred to here as if it were unemployment, to be consistent with other papers discussed.

The relation used is logarithmic in both variables, similar to that used by Phillips for one variable in his study. No negative values of the variables occur. The results generally support the hypothesis tested. Leaving out the years before 1950 on the basis that a deliberate policy of wage restraint made them unsuitable, the authors find both the price and unemployment terms are significant in explaining the wage changes that occurred. The coefficient of the price term is near 0.5, indicating that a given percentage change in prices, while significant, is associated with only one half that percentage change in wages. On the other hand, the unemployment term has considerable leverage, with a change of about one point in the percentage unemployment being associated with a change of 3 or 4 percentage points in the annual rate of wage change. In addition, the authors associate an autonomous annual wage increase of $2\frac{1}{2}$ percent with their constant term.

In studying broad individual industries, the results are parallel for the most part to those in the aggregated study. The most interesting result of this part of the paper is that aggregate unemployment does about as well in explaining wage changes in individual industries as do the unemployment figures for the individual industries themselves. The authors offer two possible explanations for this. First, they reason that the level of aggregate unemployment might affect the general "climate" of wage negotiations, with the economic situation of different industries being of much less importance. Alternatively, they suggest this result may reflect a situation with general wages determined by the pattern of wages in one or more "wage-leader" industries, while unemployment in these industries is highly correlated with aggregate unemployment.

The first explanation seems too loose to lend itself to examination, although a more "economic" argument might be made embodying somewhat the same view. The second argument, that "wage-leader" industries exist which determine the terms of wage settlements to be applied elsewhere, is a conjecture that has been expressed often. In the present case, if the argument given were true, lagged values of the explanatory aggregate variables should explain wage changes in the "follower" industries, with the size of the lag depending on the amount of time elapsing since the settlement in the leader industry. The authors report no such finding.

### L. R. Klein and R. J. Ball

One final study[12] of the British case deserves mention here since, in contrast to the other works we have discussed, it explicitly considers the wage relation in the context of a system of simultaneous equations. This study, authored by L. R. Klein and R. J. Ball, is an offshoot of work done on an econometric model of the United Kingdom economy as a whole. The wage- and price-determining subsystem of the larger model was considered by the authors sufficiently self-contained to warrant separate consideration.

The period covered is 1948–1957, and quarterly observations are used throughout. Four equations are used, of which the first is of principal interest to us. It relates annual wage changes to unemployment, price changes, and a dummy variable reflecting a presumed change in the attitudes of trade unions after 1952. Unemployment enters the relation linearly in contrast to the nonlinear forms used in the other studies discussed here. The authors use simple first differences as their wage-change and price-change variables rather than the corresponding percentage changes. This procedure seems questionable since the unemployment rate is a trendless variable, while wages and prices have definite rising trends throughout the period studied. The effect of this is to associate a given rate of unemployment with say a 10 percent increase in wages at one time, but only a 5 percent increase at some later time when wages have doubled. One way in which this formulation may have prejudiced the results will be discussed.

The method of estimation used is limited-information maximum likelihood. This method avoids the problem of biased estimates which would arise with simple least-squares estimates of the wage equation if in fact this equation were part of a nonrecursive system. The system specified by Klein and Ball is nonrecursive. The authors of the other studies discussed here use simple least-squares estimates but generally argue that the lags involved in their specifications make this technique tolerable.

The results of interest here are those for the wage equation. The coefficients for price change, unemployment, and trade union attitude are all significant. The main apparent difference from the results of the other studies seems to be in the very high coefficient for the price-change term. This coefficient is 0.85 using an index of

[12] Klein, L. R., and R. J. Ball, "Some Econometrics of Determination of Absolute Prices and Wages," *Economic Journal*, Vol. 69 (September 1959).

price changes over the two years preceding a wage change, and 0.98 using an index involving only price changes corresponding to the year over which the wage change is measured. The authors interpret these coefficients near unity to mean the wage-rate adjustment to price changes roughly compensates for the effects of price increases.[13] But this finding is in conflict with the results of the other studies, just cited, over the same period. Lipsey reports a coefficient of 0.69, which he revises in a footnote to about 0.50. Dicks-Mireaux and Dow report a coefficient of near 0.5. There are two reasons why the Klein and Ball result may be too high. The first is that wages have risen somewhat more than prices, so that the elasticity of wages with respect to prices is lower than their price coefficient. This is because the price coefficient comes from a regression using first differences of wages and prices rather than percentage changes. The second reason comes from biasing the coefficient of unemployment by not treating wages as percentage changes. If in fact percentage changes are the appropriate form to specify, then using first differences instead will decrease the fit with unemployment, which is trendless, and bias the unemployment coefficient. And in this circumstance, the coefficient of price changes may be biased upward as well. The other studies use percentage changes rather than first differences in the wage and price variables so that neither of these two comments apply to them, and this may explain the difference in results.

Klein and Ball also estimate their wage equation with simple least squares. A comparison of these estimates with those using the limited-information maximum-likelihood technique on all four equations is interesting. With least squares, the unemployment coefficient is 0.089 and that of prices is 0.812. With the consistent estimation technique, the corresponding figures are 0.091 and 0.854. The two methods of estimation give virtually indistinguishable results.

The authors experiment further with a wage equation including additional explanatory variables, thus attempting the more general specification of the wage relation argued for here. The two additional variables tried are average labor productivity and profits. The first of these has a negative coefficient and is insignificant. The second has a significant positive coefficient, but the authors reject it on the grounds that it is too highly correlated with the other explanatory variables and its influence is already reflected in them.

[13] *Ibid.*, p. 473.

They do not present the results of a regression using profits, so it is not possible to comment carefully on their treatment.

## Recent Studies for the American Economy

### William G. Bowen

All the foregoing studies have dealt with the British economy. The most ambitious attempt thus far to examine the American experience is William G. Bowen's book,[14] published in 1960. It deals with several questions connected with the wage change-unemployment relation. Is there such a relation? Is it changing over time? What is the effect of variables such as the direction of change of unemployment, changes in employment, the level of profits, prices, unionization, and industrial concentration? In expanding the problem by inquiring into the effect of factors other than unemployment, Bowen moves toward the kind of analysis argued for here. Indeed, by considering some variables that must be dealt with cross-sectionally, he addresses important questions that are beyond the scope of the present study, which is confined to an aggregated analysis over time. On the other hand, in looking at such a wide range of issues, he employs methods that limit the power of the analysis. In particular, his approach does not reflect the simultaneous interaction of several factors in determining wages, and it fails to provide a quantitative estimate of the impact on wages of differing unemployment rates. Nonetheless, the study is comprehensive in many respects, and it offers several conclusions that deserve discussion here.

Roughly, Bowen's approach is to look at unemployment as the main explanatory variable of interest and then look for ways to explain irregularities in this basic relationship. He starts with an introductory look at the whole twentieth century, using annual wage changes for manufacturing production workers and unemployment for the nonfarm economy. By calculating median wage changes for various unemployment levels, he finds a very slight and highly erratic connection. But the same technique seems to show a perverse relation for the post-World War II years; the higher unemployment is, the faster wages rise. Despite the doubtful nature of these results, Bowen concludes that in the postwar period there has been an increase in the rate at which wages rise for given levels of unemployment compared with the years before the war.

[14] Bowen, William G., *Wage Behavior in the Post War Period—An Empirical Analysis* (Princeton, N. J.: Princeton University Press, 1960).

For the detailed look at the postwar years, Bowen is on sounder ground. The data are available monthly and he uses this to separate his observations into subperiods according to the prevailing level of unemployment. He distinguishes between the three postwar recession periods and the three prosperity periods in between, using the 4.3 percent unemployment level as the dividing line. The recessions are further divided into their contraction and recovery periods. The average rates of wage change for each period are then compared.

The results indicate that unemployment and wage changes are related in the way one would have expected. The average rate of wage change in the recession periods is 3.9 percent and in the prosperity periods, 6.3 percent. Furthermore, in the recession periods, the contraction phases show a lower average wage increase than do the recovery phases.

Bowen tries several other variables to explain the differences between the wage changes observed in the three prosperity as opposed to the three recession periods. To test the role of profits, he computes the average profit rate over each subperiod. This he compares with the wage changes that occurred, and concludes that profits add nothing to the explanation. He treats employment, price changes, and the existence of long-term contracts in a similar way and decides that the last two help explain the large wage increase of the 1958 recession.

In all, it seems that better use could be made of the available data. The reduction of monthly unemployment figures into a few broad categories is descriptively useful, but throws away a great deal of information. The same is true of the treatment given to profits and price changes. Furthermore, nowhere is the simultaneous interaction of these, and possibly other, variables given close examination. It would seem valuable to have regressions made on these variables with coefficients and standard errors given. On the other hand, Bowen's results do provide evidence that the expected relation between wage changes and unemployment exists.

In addition to the aggregated study of all manufacturing, Bowen disaggregates wage changes into the 2-digit industry groups defined by the 1947 Standard Industrial Classification. Again using the unemployment subperiods just defined, he does a cross-section analysis of the relation between wage changes and other variables characterizing each industry for the different subperiods. Disaggregation in such a study is full of problems, and Bowen's treatment may be as useful as any. But apart from conceptual problems in disaggregating, it still has the drawback mentioned of throwing away information by dealing with average values over subperiods taken to be homogeneous with respect to unemployment. The four explanatory variables used to characterize each industry in each unemployment subperiod are employment, profit rate, degree of industrial concentration, and degree of labor organization. The analysis consists essentially of calculating partial correlations of these variables with the wage changes observed in each industry. For the most part, the results are slightly ambiguous, with no variables standing out in all subperiods. Broadly, wage changes are parallel in all industries in the various unemployment subperiods. High aggregate unemployment holds back wage increases in all industries, and periods of national prosperity result in large wage increases throughout. However, some interesting differences are found, even if they require careful searching. In two of the three subperiods when general unemployment is low, industries increasing employment rapidly show larger wage increases than the average. There is evidence also that high unionization has a positive effect on wage increase in two of the three boom periods, while highly concentrated industries show above-average wage increases in two of the three recession subperiods. Finally, industries which are both highly unionized and concentrated have a general tendency for larger than average wage increases over the whole period studied. However, this last result is clouded by the fact that the profit rate as a variable (in place of high concentration and unionization) would give about the same results.

### Rattan J. Bhatia

In two separate articles, Rattan J. Bhatia has also studied factors affecting wages in the United States. In the first,[15] Bhatia tests Phillips' hypothesis[16] that the level and rate of change of unemployment will largely explain the rate of change of wages. In the second,[17] he tries profits and the change in profits as alternative explanatory variables.

The first paper examines the entire twentieth century except for

[15] Bhatia, Rattan J., "Unemployment and the Rate of Change of Money Earnings in the United States 1900–1958," *Economica*, Vol. XXVIII (August 1961).

[16] Phillips, A. W., *op. cit.*

[17] Bhatia, Rattan J., "Profits and the Rate of Change in Money Earnings in the United States, 1935–1959," *Economica*, Vol. XXIX (August 1962).

a few years which are considered nonrepresentative. The only explanatory variable used explicitly is unemployment, although price changes are considered to the extent that years marked by very sharp price increases (1916–1919) are excluded. In general, Bhatia finds very little support for the hypothesis that unemployment explains wage changes. For the earlier years, 1900–1932, he finds some relation, but considers it very loose. From 1935 to 1941, again there is some connection, but one he considers unsatisfactory. And from 1948 to 1958, he finds even less connection than in the previous periods. For all his periods, Bhatia finds no connection of wage changes with the rate of change in unemployment, although this variable is never actually used in a regression equation. Unfortunately, Bhatia does not give enough of his results to make possible any investigation of why they arise. However, at least two questions may be raised about the study. One is whether there might not be much more information about the role of unemployment and about the role of other variables if they were included simultaneously in a statistical analysis. The second is whether monthly or quarterly data might not sharpen the analysis of the post-World War II period. The annual data used, although they have to do for the more distant past, may not be sharp enough for the analysis attempted. The strong differences in the conclusions reached by Bhatia and Bowen are not consistent with each other, and one must suspect blunt tools are the source of the disagreements.

The second paper deals mainly with the post-World War II period, although some results are then extended back to 1935. It is apparently prompted by an article of Nicholas Kaldor,[18] which includes as part of its theoretical argument the opinion that a rise in the profits of one period leads to a rise in the wages of the next. The hypothesis that Bhatia chooses to test is that the change in wages can be explained by the level and change of the rate of profits. He concludes that this relation does hold and is far more satisfactory than unemployment for explaining wage changes. However, the comparison is not a fair one since, in this second paper, *monthly* data for profits and wages are used, which may explain the better results.

The percentage rate of return on equity before taxes is used to measure profits, although the author points out that other measures would give similar results. In fact, because of the excess profits tax

[18] Kaldor, Nicholas, "Economic Growth and the Problem of Inflation," *Economica*, N.S. 26 (November 1959).

of the Korean War and the rapid rise of all monetary variables in that period, profits after tax would probably not fit as well, although the after-tax concept may be conceptually more acceptable.

Different lags are tried, and a two-month lag gives the best results. For this case, the level and rate of change of profits explain wage changes in a regression with a squared correlation coefficient of 0.80. Both explanatory variables are significant. The analysis is extended to the period 1935 to 1948, but the strikingly good fit of the postwar years is not repeated. Changes in profits are not significant, and the optimal lag increases to six months. The domination of this period by World War II probably makes the results very uncertain.

The strong results in favor of profits as an explanatory variable again point up the contrast with Bowen's conclusion that profits do not help explain postwar aggregate wage behavior. Bhatia makes no attempt to include both profits and unemployment in his analysis nor, for that matter, any other variables.

As with the other studies discussed, it is this commitment to one main explanatory variable at a time that is unsatisfactory. If wage rates are influenced by several economic variables, it is important to consider their simultaneous interaction. This is no less true if interest centers on the relation between one of these variables and wage changes. Most of the studies, Bhatia's last one excepted, have centered on the relation between wage changes and unemployment. In the present work, this relation will also be of primary interest since it is directly relevant to the inflation-unemployment problem faced by the economy. But in order to study this relation, it will be necessary to specify the wage-determination equation fully and to estimate the simultaneous effect of all the relevant explanatory variables.

# 2

# A Model of Aggregate
# Wage Determination

## Introduction

In this chapter, the relationship between wage changes and certain
key explanatory variables are discussed and then used to formulate
a one-equation model for explaining changes in aggregate average
wage levels. In Chapters 3 and 4, the parameters from several variations of this basic wage-determination equation are estimated for
different periods and the implications of these estimates are examined in detail.

## The Use of Aggregate Relationships

Formulating a model to explain price changes in a broad market
can be difficult. If the price in question is the wage rate for labor, it
can be especially treacherous. Labor is a heterogeneous commodity
in its economic characteristics such as skills. It is not easily trans-
portable. To the extent that knowledge of a job makes a worker
more useful, employed labor represents an investment by the employer. Requirements of human dignity surround the purchase and
sale of labor services with special problems not associated with
other commodities. And, perhaps most important for the analyst,
the world of collective bargaining creates supply conditions that
are specific to the labor market.

Some of these special characteristics are suitable subjects for
analysis in themselves. But in a fairly aggregated study such as this
one, some must be assumed away or disregarded and others taken
account of indirectly. The aim must be to isolate factors of sufficient

importance to show through the necessary compromises with the microeconomic detail.

In this study, a single average wage rate is always the variable to be explained. The same model is used to estimate equations explaining wage changes in all manufacturing and in the subgroups of durable-goods and nondurable-goods industries within manufacturing. Through the choice of a single wage variable and fairly high levels of cross-industry aggregation, the existence of heterogeneous labor supply is largely disregarded.

The lack of any distinction among different job categories or skill levels in this procedure poses no great difficulties. Although over time some change may occur in the relative wages of one skill group over another, the dominant pattern is for all groups within an industry to move together. This is due not only to the fact that the same economic forces operate on the demand for all forms of labor within an industry but also to the institutional character of labor unions, which generally negotiate along industry lines and therefore simultaneously represent production workers of all skill levels and job categories.

Aggregation across industry lines into the broader categories of durable- and nondurable-goods industries and all manufacturing is a different problem, although again the procedure seems acceptable. There are two ways in which differences among industries could arise. The first is if wages in each industry reacted similarly to the same economic forces, but these forces were in fact different in magnitude in the different industries at various times. In other words, each industry might be characterized by the same relation expressing wage changes as a function of other variables; but the explanatory variables might have different values for each industry at any one time, thus resulting in different observed wage behavior for each industry. Ignoring the stochastic nature of the relation, this can be written as

$$w_i = f(X_i), \qquad (2.1)$$

where $w$ is used to stand for the rate of wage change and where the subscript refers to the $i$th industry and $X$ is a vector of explanatory variables. The second way for interindustry differences to arise is for wages in different industries to react differently to the same economic forces; or, in other words, for each industry to have different parameters in its relation expressing wage changes as a function of other variables. In symbols, this proposition asserts that

$$w_i = f_i(X), \qquad (2.2)$$

where now the subscript on $f$ denotes a different relation between $w$ and the vector $X$ for each industry.

The second case can be taken care of formally, if somewhat trivially, by including in the list of explanatory variables all those characteristics that made the functions for the several industries differ from each other. Often these missing explanatory variables are institutional characteristics that are hard to quantify. For instance, two variables often mentioned in trying to account for interindustry differences in manufacturing are the strength of unions and the degree of concentration existing in the product markets. Examining the effect of such variables is an important task for economists, full of useful implications for policy as well as theory. And despite the serious difficulties involved, many have tried to tackle the problem.[1] But there are equally useful questions to ask about the effect of other economic forces, and these may lend themselves to a more aggregated study.

In general, if differences of the second kind discussed are ignored, it is appropriate to aggregate. For in this case, the disaggregated units are each characterized by the same function relating the variable to be explained, in our case wage changes, to the explanatory variables, and we have the first case described by Equation 2.1. If the function represents a linear relation, it then follows that

$$w = f(X), \qquad (2.3)$$

where the variables without subscripts are aggregates. Basically, this is the situation assumed in this study. The variables used to explain wage behavior at the level of aggregation used in the empirical analysis are either by their nature aggregates or else highly correlated among the different industries or other subgroups to which the analysis might be applied. This minimizes the chance of serious errors arising from aggregation if the relationships of wage changes to some explanatory variables are in fact not linear.[2]

---

[1] For an example in the present context of wage behavior, see William G. Bowen, *Wage Behavior in the Post War Period–An Empirical Analysis* (Princeton, N. J.: Princeton University Press, 1960).

[2] These paragraphs do not attempt to deal rigorously with the general issue of estimating aggregated relations and the properties of the parameter estimates that are obtained. Under reasonable conditions which the assumptions made above implicitly assume are approximated here, these estimates will be unbiased. A thorough discussion of the question is given by Henri Theil, *The Linear Aggregation of Economic Relations* (Amsterdam: North Holland Publishing Co., 1954).

## A Model of Wage Determination

The purely competitive model affords a starting point for examining the factors affecting wages. Assume labor service is a homogeneous good and its price is the wage rate. Since well-defined supply and demand curves exist, the equilibrium wage is the one at which there is no excess demand (either positive or negative) for labor. If a positive excess demand exists, the wage will not be an equilibrium one, and unsatisfied employers will bid it up until the excess demand disappears. Similarly, if the quantity of labor offered exceeds that demanded at a given wage, the wage will fall in order to wipe out the negative excess demand.[3] Price theory is less clear about how fast the adjustment of a price to a new equilibrium level will be, but the general assumption is that the speed of adjustment is proportional to the amount of excess demand. Percentage unemployment immediately suggests itself as a measure of the excess demand for labor. The two are closely related, although not linearly. With this measure, zero excess demand would be associated with a positive amount of unemployment representing the condition in which the number of job vacancies equals the number of workers looking for jobs. For higher rates of unemployment, excess demand would be negative. For lower unemployment percentages, excess demand would be positive; and as unemployment approached zero, excess demand would become indefinitely large. Under this interpretation, price theory suggests that the rate of change of wages would be proportional to a nonlinear function of the rate of unemployment.

One fault with a model that adheres strictly to these lines of competitive price theory is that it leaves no room for any other explanatory variables, however plausible they may seem on intuitive grounds or however well they may perform in empirical tests. If the rate of wage change is proportional to the amount of excess demand which in turn is measured by unemployment, there is no room for other variables. All economic forces must act on either the demand for or supply of labor, and their effect is already measured by unemployment. Explaining real wages in such a model does introduce

---

[3] This treatment in terms of a competitive wage model and the following discussion of unemployment as a measure of excess demand is very close to Lipsey's in his article, "The Relation Between Unemployment and the Rate of Change of Money Wage Rates in the United Kingdom, 1862–1957: A Further Analysis," *Economica*, N.S. 27 (February 1960).

living costs as a variable affecting money wages, but with a fixed elasticity of one.

If this seems too restrictive a model, some part of the previous argument must be changed. Either the theory of adjustment must be modified or the assumption of perfect competition dropped. In fact, both can be done comfortably in the problem at hand with some confidence that we will be moving toward a more accurate specification of the wage-determining process. The importance of unemployment in determining wage behavior seems plausible enough. The difficulty lies not in having come this far but in not going further.

Even a casual view of many labor markets suggests the competitive model is too weak an approximation to use slavishly here. And with imperfect markets the equilibrium wage will not even be one that equates the supply and demand for labor. A monopsonist employer will try to pay wages such that his own demands for labor at that wage are not satisfied. A monopolist union will bargain for a wage level that leaves willing potential employees out of work. It is hard to reject *a priori* the possibility that factors other than the unemployment rate affect the speed of adjustment in wages, if, indeed, not the equilibrium level of wages itself. And it seems unnecessarily restrictive to assume from the start that real rather than money wages are the appropriate variable to explain, when one of the most interesting questions in this area is the degree to which living costs directly affect wages. A model that acknowledges these points should yield more useful results, although it will necessarily represent a somewhat looser theoretical abstraction than the competitive case.

The most realistic picture of the wage-setting institutions in manufacturing as a whole would undoubtedly include the whole spectrum of degrees of market power. In a few cases, the purely competitive model outlined earlier might apply. At the other extreme, some wage bargains would be made under conditions of virtual bilateral monopoly. In between would be various combinations of strong and weak labor bargaining units facing employers with different degrees of monopoly power in their product markets and monopsony power as hirers of labor. A theory explaining the behavior of aggregate wages could not hope to encompass specifically all the different microeconomic theories of wage behavior associated with these cases. But it need not do so to be effective for the present purpose. The problem may be intrinsically a macroeconomic one in the sense at the appropriate variables to explain changes in the general wage level may be aggregate ones, with any hypotheses about behavioral underpinnings at a microeconomic level affording no additional information. Even if this is not the case, one can discuss the impact of those key variables that should be important in most of the labor market and product market situations. These variables are the level of unemployment, the rate of profits, changes in the cost of living, and the state of expectations.

## The Level of Unemployment

As a measure of the excess demand for labor, the unemployment rate is the first variable used for explaining wage changes. In nearly competitive labor markets the previous argument applies, and an appropriate hypothesis would be that the rate of change of wages is a function simply of the unemployment rate. Since at least some wages are determined under approximately these conditions, this itself would justify the use of unemployment as one of the explanatory variables of changes in an aggregate wage level. But excess demand is important in other labor markets as well.

Collective bargaining is the system under which most wages in the manufacturing sector are set. Under this system, the amount of excess demand in the labor market at the time a wage contract is being negotiated will have an effect on the wage settlement ultimately reached. Consider the case of a tight labor market — that is, one with large excess demand. Under this condition, employers are willing to grant especially large wage increases for at least three reasons. First, they are particularly anxious to avoid a strike which would completely frustrate their need for labor. Here the high level of their demand is one indicator of the disutility of a strike to the employers. Second, since the demand for labor is derived from the demand for the output of the firm, these conditions also are associated with a maximum ability to pass on the costs of higher wages in the form of higher prices. This is not an assertion that individual firms can profitably raise prices as they wish. But in a world of imperfect competition with sticky prices, their ability to do so is greatest when they are operating in a sellers' market. And third, a high level of demand for labor means that at least some employers may be trying to increase their employment by bidding labor away from others, and so may be willing to raise their wages quite apart from whether labor demanded it.

The relevant market area over which unemployment should be

measured is, for some parts of the argument, geographically small as far as the effect of unemployment on wages is concerned. There is only one consideration based on a broad measure of unemployment: that a strong demand for labor is associated with strong product demand. The other reasons for expecting a relationship between wage changes and unemployment are based on local labor market conditions. Labor moves to places offering better employment opportunities only in response to long-run opportunity differentials, and even then there may be considerable immobility as the existence of certain depressed areas indicates. The significance of this to the present argument is that the unemployment concept relevant for explaining individual wage bargains is partly a broad one, determined by industries whose products are in strong (or weak) demand, and partly a narrow geographic one, determined by local labor market conditions. In practice, however, the local distinctions cited become blurred. Owing to the interrelations of a modern economy, aggregate demand generally varies in a similar manner over most industries and areas. Also, bargaining by some of the largest unions may simultaneously involve workers in widely separated geographic areas whose unemployment situations may not be identical, suggesting that an average is the governing value. Recently, work has been done by Kalachek and others establishing the close tie between the aggregate unemployment rate and unemployment among various subgroups in the population.[4] Such findings strengthen the case for dealing with an aggregate unemployment measure here.

## The Cost of Living

The cost of living is perhaps the most obvious factor affecting wages, although not necessarily the most important. It is obvious, at least in recent times, because so many wage contracts include cost-of-living clauses that automatically change basic wage rates according to changes in an index of living costs.[5] The measure almost universally used is the Consumer Price Index compiled by the

[4] Kalachek, Edward, "The Determinants of Higher Unemployment Rates, 1958–60," Unpublished doctoral dissertation, Massachusetts Institute of Technology, Cambridge, Mass., 1963.

[5] Since the Korean War, when cost-of-living clauses became popular, roughly 20 percent of all workers covered by collective bargaining agreements have had their wages tied to such clauses, except in a few periods when their popularity waned. Source: *Monthly Labor Review*, issues of March 1955, January 1957, and December 1960.

Bureau of Labor Statistics. Although not perfect, it gives a close and widely accepted measure of living costs and will be used in this paper.

Apart from those wages covered by cost-of-living clauses, a change in the Consumer Price Index affects wages owing to the asymmetrical impact it has on employer and enployee. In a situation of collective bargaining, rising living costs strengthen the union side in its claims for wage increases and put the union under increasing pressure from its members to get them. The rise in the Index creates no offsetting change in the resistance to an increase on the employer's part, so on balance the effect favors higher wages. There are independent studies which have explored the importance of price changes to wage bargaining and generally fortified these observations.[6]

There are two reasons why the cost of living has such a strong effect on the attitude of workers and hence on the strength of their union's bargaining position. The first is that changes in living costs have an obvious and direct effect on the welfare of workers, precisely symmetrical to changes in their money wages. While the maximum awareness may be of the money size of a paycheck, there is also considerable sensitivity to how much this paycheck will buy. Indeed, the general climate of discussion about inflation may even serve to overemphasize the extent to which prices rise. The discontent with prices implied in all the reminiscing about "the good old days" often seems to exaggerate the actual drop in purchasing power. The second reason why living costs are an important variable serves to amplify the first. The Consumer Price Index is such a ready measure of living costs that unions can easily use a rise in the Index to rally the membership or confront the industry with the need for larger wage changes. Thus not only does discontent originate with the workers and their unions when prices rise but the Index itself becomes a weapon at the bargaining table.

Under collective bargaining, the wage settlement depends upon the relative pressure and resistance exerted by the two parties, and it is this feature that gives rise to the importance of cost-of-living changes just described. But many of the same forces operate in the

[6] One striking example is given by W. S. Woytinsky, who found that 84.2 percent of unions responding to questioning mentioned cost-of-living changes as the most important wage criterion in their postwar negotiations. Even making allowances for the difference between what people say and what really counts, this response is impressive. W. S. Woytinsky, *Labor and Management Look at Collective Bargaining* (New York: Twentieth Century Fund, 1949), p. 73.

case of unorganized workers as well. To the extent that an employer is willing to pay something to avoid discontent among his workers, the effect of rising prices will be similar under this form of wage determination. And, as in all parts of the argument, factors operating on wage bargains in unionized industries will exert influence indirectly on wages elsewhere through competition among employers.

Although this discussion has been mainly in terms of rising prices, there is probably a similar effect when living costs fall, although possibly not as strong. Thus, while a rising Consumer Price Index affords labor a strong argument for a larger wage increase, business can be expected to use the Index as a weapon for moderation in wage settlements at times when prices have been relatively stable. And the other effects described similarly cut in both directions. As only one variable in the explanation of wage changes, falling prices to consumers need not lead to falling wages. All that one would expect is that the resulting wage change would be smaller than otherwise, other things being equal. Since the observations available are dominated by increases in the Consumer Price Index, it is hard to test whether falling prices have a smaller proportional effect than do rising prices, and it will not be assumed that this is the case.

### Profits

The third variable whose effect on wages will be examined is profits, or better, some measure of profitability. Some writers go so far as to put all the weight of explaining wages on such a variable, although the argument for this has never been put forth convincingly in my opinion. Bhatia[7] apparently takes this position in his recent empirical paper, and Kaldor[8] makes this assertion as part of a broader theoretical model.

Kaldor assumes that wages are all set by collective bargaining and therefore wage settlements depend on the relative bargaining strength of labor. But he then argues further that relative strength at the bargaining table, and hence the resulting wage rate, depends solely on profits, or more precisely, on last year's profits, since that is all either party knows about. He specifically rejects the cost of living as a factor and considers unemployment as unimportant, it being only incidentally correlated with wage changes through its

[7] Bhatia, Rattan J., "Profits and the Rate of Change in Money Earnings in the United States, 1935–1959," *Economica*, Vol. XXIX (August 1962).

[8] Kaldor, Nicholas, "Economic Growth and the Problem of Inflation," *Economica*, N.S. 26 (November 1959).

correlation with profits, the true explanatory variable.[9] Since Kaldor is not addressing himself mainly to the question of wage determination, he does not elaborate on these assertions. Their correctness is not obvious, and profits here will be treated as just one of the factors affecting wages. If Kaldor's position is right, it should come out in the tests on the data.

In the present model, the aspect of the bargaining situation most clearly identified with profits is the ability of employers to pay a given wage increase. It may not be entirely clear that profits are an appropriate measure of this ability. For instance, if wage changes in a firm lead to price changes for the output of the firm, all or part of a wage change may ultimately be paid for, in some sense, through increased prices. As the ability of a firm to pass on wage increases changes, say through a change in its degree of monopoly power or in the prices of competing products, so too would its resistance to a wage increase. But the first of these is a long-run effect of little importance here; and the second would surely show up in the profits of the firm in question, although imperfectly. More to the point, however, the use of profits is not meant to capture all the dimensions of a firm's ability to grant a wage increase. Rather, the fact that this ability is partially reflected in profits is one of the reasons for expecting profits to help explain wage changes.

Since the various calls on the profits of a firm depend roughly on the amount of its equity capital, its ability to meet them is measured by the ratio of profits to equity rather than simple profits. This ratio, the profit rate, will be the variable used in this study.

In addition to the direct impact of the profit rate through the ability to pay, it also measures another factor influencing the wage bargain. Stubborn resistance by both sides in a collective bargaining dispute will lead to a strike, the principal weapon and threat of organized workers. The profit rate indicates the cost to the firm, at given wage rates, of closing down operations during a strike. For a time, the firm may be able to meet sales out of inventories, especially when inventories are high and sales slow. At such times, a firm is least vulnerable to a strike and may even welcome work stoppage for a time. But in boom times, when profits are highest, the ability to operate out of inventories is limited.

The profit rate not only affects the outcome of wage negotiations by its influence on management's ability to pay and reluctance to

---

[9] *Ibid.*, p. 294.

incur work stoppages, it also affects wage negotiations through the reactions of workers and possibly even the general public. Since the effectiveness of unions in negotiating for wage changes depends on the backing of the workers they represent, factors acting to convince workers that they deserve a certain settlement will enhance the bargaining strength of a union. A change in the cost of living is such a factor, and so is the profit rate. Profit figures are easily available and can be used to influence worker opinion. On occasional instances when an important negotiation is widely publicized, the pressure of public opinion may be still another factor in the outcome, and again profits may be an important variable in shaping this opinion.

The role of profits has been discussed in the context of wages set by collective bargaining. Most of the points made are relevant chiefly to this form of wage determination since they involve the resistance or pressure exerted by the two sides. The ability-to-pay argument is more general since it affects firms involved in unilateral wage setting as well. The impact of profits in all the arguments is consistently in one direction, with higher profit rates leading to larger wage increases.

### The State of Expectations

Up to now, the *level* of two important variables, profit rate and unemployment, has been discussed. But wage changes may also be influenced by the *direction* in which these variables are moving. The main reason for using directions or rates of change as explanatory variables is that they represent a basis for prediction. For instance, if falling profits lead to expectations of still lower levels, and if this expectation affects wage bargaining, then the change in profits ought to be included as an explanatory variable.

If indicators of the direction in which key variables are moving are used on this basis, there arises the question of which variable to use. Both the level of unemployment and the profit rate are included in this study; and measures of the change in unemployment and the change in profits have been used by others, although not together. The case for choosing is not so clear as with levels, for if predictions are influenced at all, it is by changes in any measure of activity that is either publicized or to which the parties themselves are sensitive. Thus the opinion that unemployment would rise, or gross national product would fall, could affect a firm's profit estimate in the same way as the information that profits last quarter had fallen relative to a year earlier. Since both unemployment and profit rate are used in this study, indicators of the change in each are also used in an initial formulation; and a selection is then made on the basis of empirical results.

## The Model To Be Tested

In this section, the relationships suggested by the preceding discussion will be translated into a form suitable for empirical estimation in the next chapter. Since wage determination in the manufacturing sector is dominated institutionally by collective bargaining, the forces operating in a bargaining situation have been the point of reference for much of the previous argument. Formally, this will also be the case in the model to be developed here, although no important mis-specifications are involved because other forms of wage setting are also present.

Assume that wages everywhere are set annually and let $W_t$ be the prevailing average wage rate in period $t$. For those wages negotiated in a given quarter, designated $W_t^*$ (or unilaterally changed by employers in that quarter), the quarterly percentage wage change is

$$\frac{W_t^* - W_{t-1}^*}{W_{t-1}^*}. \tag{2.4}$$

The size of this wage change will depend on the prevailing economic conditions relevant to the wage settlements, described by explanatory variables which for now will simply be specified as the vector $x_t$. Therefore,

$$\frac{W_t^* - W_{t-1}^*}{W_{t-1}^*} = ax_t + E_t \tag{2.5}$$

is the stochastic relation between the average percentage wage change in industries changing wages in a given quarter and the explanatory variables of that quarter: $E_t$ is the term for the random errors in the relation, and $ax_t$ is the cross product of the explanatory variables and their coefficients.

If wage negotiations are spread evenly throughout the year, one fourth of all wages will be negotiated in each quarter.[10] In a given

---

[10] This assumption is convenient for exposition, although much stronger than

quarter, this will result in a change in an aggregate wage index about one fourth as great as the change in those wages that were actually negotiated that quarter. The change in an aggregate wage index over a year will span four such quarters. Let $w_t$ stand for the annual percentage change in an aggregate wage index:

$$w_t = \frac{W_t - W_{t-4}}{W_{t-4}}. \tag{2.6}$$

Then $w_t$ will be approximately equal to

$$w_t = \frac{1}{4}\left( \frac{W_t^* - W_{t-1}^*}{W_{t-1}^*} + \frac{W_{t-1}^* - W_{t-2}^*}{W_{t-2}^*} + \frac{W_{t-2}^* - W_{t-3}^*}{W_{t-3}^*} \right.$$

$$\left. + \frac{W_{t-3}^* - W_{t-4}^*}{W_{t-4}} \right), \tag{2.7}$$

the average of the quarterly changes described by Equation 2.4. With Equation 2.5 as a base,

$$w_t = a(x_t + x_{t-1} + x_{t-2} + x_{t-3}) + e_t \tag{2.8}$$

now becomes the stochastic relation explaining the annual percentage change in an aggregate wage index, where $e$ is the four-quarter average of the error terms $E$. Even if $E_t$ in Equation 2.5 satisfied the usual least-squares assumptions of being normally distributed with zero mean, finite variance, and uncorrelated with the terms in $x$, the error term $e_t$ in equations such as 2.8 would not satisfy these conditions. This would not introduce asymptotic bias into least-squares estimates on Equation 2.8, but it would impair the efficiency of the estimates and produce uncertain small-sample properties for the estimates. Such statistical questions are discussed further later on, when least-squares estimates of the wage equation are made, and more thoroughly in Chapter 5 when a consistent estimating technique is used with an equation system containing a variant of the basic wage equation developed in Chapter 3.

### The Explanatory Variables

The variables in the $x$ vector of Equation 2.8 correspond to the previously discussed determinants of wage changes: the unemploy-

necessary. All that is required is that no bias exist in wage changes owing to the time of year when they take place.

ment rate, the profit rate, the change in the cost of living, the change in profit rate, and the direction in which unemployment is changing.

The unemployment rate is measured separately for durable-goods industries, nondurable-goods industries, and the entire civilian labor force, although data for the first two of these pose conceptual problems that limit their reliability. They are used in making estimates with the corresponding wage-rate concepts, and these wage rates are also estimated using the broader unemployment series. The form used for the unemployment variable is discussed in Chapter 3 when that variable is introduced. One may note here that nonlinear forms, $U^{-1}$ and $U^{-2}$, are used. An approximation is therefore involved in the aggregation from Equations 2.5 to 2.8 since the inverse of average unemployment is not quite the same thing as the average of the inverse of unemployment. But the difference is slight and is ignored.

The profit rate is also measured at three levels of aggregation: durable-goods industries, nondurable-goods industries, and all manufacturing. It is used in the linear form of the variable.

Two versions of the variable for cost-of-living changes are tried. One involves quarterly price changes, the other annual price changes. In both cases the variables enter in linear form.

The last variables tried measure the direction of movement of broad aggregates in the economy. One is a dummy for the direction in which unemployment is moving. The other is the first difference of profit rate.

All the preceding variables are used as four-quarter averages or sums, which are the forms appropriate to Equation 2.8. They are discussed more fully as they are used in Chapter 3, and in the appendix, which describes the sources of data and construction of the series used in this study and presents the data in the principal series that are used.

### Departures from the Annual Wage-Change Model

There are two kinds of effects on wages that do not fit directly into the model described here. These arise from contract clauses, such as for adjustments to the cost of living, that affect wages more often than at annual negotiations; and the existence of long-term contracts which cause some wages to change less often than at annual intervals.

The first of these presents no problem. The effect on wage increases from the cost-of-living clause is simply absorbed into the $x$ vectors in Equation 2.8. The aggregation from Equation 2.5 up to Equation 2.8 may be thought of as including one fourth of the change in negotiated wages for each quarter plus a linear function of changes in the cost of living. Since all explanatory variables are treated as linear functions of wage change, the cost of living is directly absorbed in the $x$ vectors when aggregating up to Equation 2.8. (As a matter of notation, the $x$ vectors in that equation should now have a new designation.)

The effect of long-term contracts is less directly encompassed in the formulation used here. However, under fairly reasonable assumptions, their presence will not bias the results. What is necessary is that the incidence of negotiations on long-term contracts is not correlated with economic conditions affecting wages; and that for given economic conditions, wages set under these contracts have the same expected value over the life of the contract as do wages set under shorter contracts over the same period. Neither of these assumptions seems unreasonable. There are undoubtedly cases of long-term contracts that were signed at particularly advantageous times for one or the other bargaining parties. The automobile workers' contract in 1955 and the electrical workers' contract in 1961 offer two examples from opposite labor-market conditions. But since either party can benefit from such an agreement if the timing is favorable, there is little reason to expect a systematic correlation of such contracts with economic conditions. Similarly most of the arguments one might think of on the second point cut both ways: long-term contracts reduce uncertainty, but for both parties; strikes are costly, but for both employer and employees. Again it seems safe to assume for the present purpose that there is no bias in either direction. With these assumptions, the presence of long-term contracts should be neutral to results with the annual model, although their presence may increase the standard error of the estimates made.[11]

[11] The possibility of using other than a one-year model was considered. Preliminary scatter diagrams were examined for longer periods, but they were less promising than the annual case.

# 3

# The Equation of Aggregate
# Wage Determination
# for the Postwar Period

**Introduction**

With a model developed expressing wage changes as a function
of several explanatory variables, it is now time to confront the model
with the data. This will test Chapter 2's hypotheses about what
factors affect wage changes and will yield quantitative estimates of
the relations involved.

In this chapter, the model is used to estimate the relation between
the rate of change of manufacturing wages and the determinants of
that rate of change during the post-World War II period. The lack
of suitable data on a broader scale limits the analysis to the manufacturing sector. However, within manufacturing it is possible to
disaggregate into the durable-goods and nondurable-goods subsectors, and most of the analysis is conducted for these subsectors as
well as for all manufacturing. Later in the study, an earlier period is
examined for comparison with the postwar results.

The estimating begins with the simple relation of unemployment
to wage changes, and then one variable at a time is added until the
full model is estimated. Working in stages this way permits comparisons along the way with the results of other studies that have
been made, and also facilitates some experimentation with different
forms and time lags for the variables used here. The data in this
chapter and in the remainder of the study are described in the appendix to this book.

## Wage Changes and Unemployment

Figure 3.1 shows a graph of the annual rate of wage change in manufacturing and in the durable-goods and nondurable-goods sub-sectors for each quarter of the postwar period covered by this study.

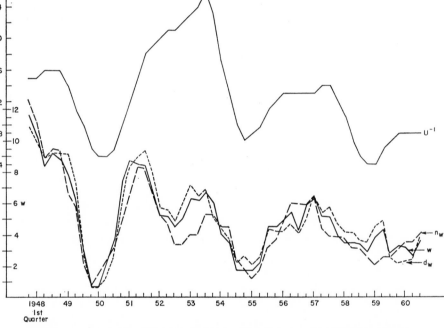

FIGURE 3.1.   *Wage changes and unemployment in the postwar period.*
Top scale: $U^{-1}$ — Inverse of average civilian labor force unemployment over last four quarters, by quarters from 1947-IV to 1960-III.
Bottom scale: $w$ — Annual percentage change in straight-time average hourly earnings, by quarters from 1947-IV to 1960-III.
Solid line: $w$ — All manufacturing industries.
Dotted line: $^{d}w$ — Durable-goods industries.
Broken line: $^{n}w$ — Nondurable-goods industries.

It also shows a graph of the inverse of the average rate of unemployment in the civilian labor force over the past four quarters for each quarter in the period. This arrangement of the data corresponds to the annual wage-change model of the last chapter.

A quick inspection of the graph suggests some tie between wage-

change and unemployment variables. But it equally suggests the
tie is only a fairly loose one, with important factors missing in the
explanation of wage movements. In the graph, the very rapid wage
increases at the start of the postwar period seem faster than unemployment rates alone suggest. On the other hand, the failure of
wage changes to follow the unemployment inverse to its peak in
1953 is equally noticeable.

Figures 3.2, 3.3, and 3.4 give the same information as Figure 3.1,

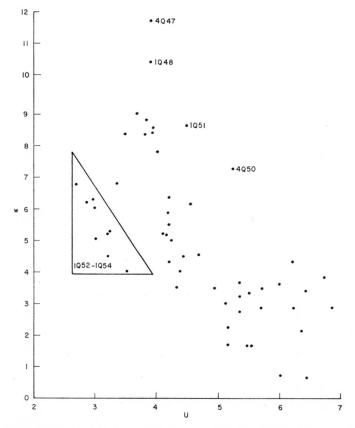

FIGURE 3.2.    *Scatter diagram of wage changes and unemployment for
all manufacturing.*
Annual percentage wage changes in manufacturing ($w_t$), versus four-
quarter average civilian labor force unemployment ($U_t$) 1947–1960,
quarterly.

but are arranged in the form of scatter diagrams showing observed percentage wage changes plotted against the corresponding unemployment rates in the civilian labor force. Figure 3.2 gives such a scatter for all manufacturing wages, while Figures 3.3 and 3.4 are for the durable-goods and nondurable-goods subsectors respectively. Again, a loose but distinct relationship appears to exist. Particularly the first and last of these scatters suggest that this wage change-unemployment relation may be a nonlinear one. Wages appear to

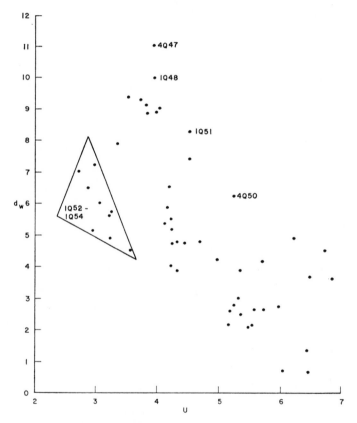

FIGURE 3.3.  *Scatter diagram of wage changes and unemployment for durable-goods industries.*

Annual percentage wage changes in durable-goods industries ($^d w_t$), versus four-quarter average of civilian labor force unemployment ($U_t$) 1947–1960, quarterly.

have some downward inflexibility that causes the curve between the two variables to flatten out at higher levels of unemployment; while at lower unemployment levels, the curve seems to rise more steeply. The previous chapter has also suggested *a priori* reasons for believing the relation to be nonlinear in about this way.

Several functional forms, linear in the parameters, can be used to accommodate the hypothesis of such a nonlinear relation. One possibility is to relate the logarithm of wage change to the logarithm

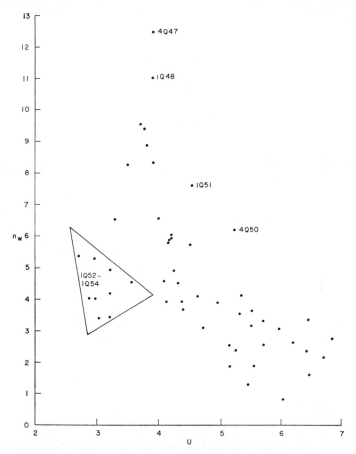

FIGURE 3.4. *Scatter diagram of wage changes and unemployment for nondurable-goods industries.*

Annual percentage wage changes in nondurable-goods industries $(^nw_t)$, versus four-quarter average of civilian labor force unemployment $(U_t)$ 1947–1960, quarterly.

of unemployment. However, as mentioned earlier, this form cannot accommodate negative values of the variables since negative logarithms are not defined. It is also objectionable for the present study because additional explanatory variables must be added as logarithms.

A general form that meets these objections is one relating wage change to a linear combination of nonlinear transformations of the unemployment variable. In particular,

$$w_t = a_1 U_t^{-1} + a_2 U_t^{-2} + a_3 U_t^{-3} + a_4 U_t^{-4} + \cdots \quad (3.1)$$

is a suitable and flexible form, where one or more of the $a_1$ coefficients may be made zero. For this study, sufficient flexibility is available using only $a_1$ and $a_2$. At a later stage, $a_2$ is also dropped without significant loss of explanatory power. The first equation estimated is therefore

$$w_t = a_0 + a_1 U_t^{-1} + a_2 U_t^{-2} + e_t, \quad (3.2)$$

where $w_t$ is an annual percentage wage change. The notation $U_t$ represents the average unemployment of the four quarters spanned by the wage change, and $e_t$ is an error term.

In this chapter and the following one, simple least-squares regressions are used to estimate the parameters of Equation 3.2 and of subsequent formulations of the wage equation. Since one of the main purposes of this part of the study is to test alternative specifications of the wage relation, it was desirable to use simple least squares in estimating. In Chapter 5, problems of statistical methodology and the possibility of bias in the least-squares estimates are considered. Anticipating the discussion of that chapter, it appears the present conclusions reached with simple least-squares estimates require no serious modifications.

The least-squares regression on Equation 3.2 for all manufacturing industries yields

$$w_t = -2.916 + 45.197 \, U_t^{-1} - 47.807 \, U_t^{-2} + e_t, \quad (3.3)$$
$$(13.189) \qquad\qquad (26.936)$$

where the standard errors of the coefficient estimates are given below them in parenthesis.[1] The fraction of variation explained by this regression, $R^2$, is 0.498.

[1] The ratio $a_i - a_i^* / \text{S.E.}$ of $a_i$ is assumed to have a $t$ distribution, where $a_i$ is the estimated coefficient value and $a_i^*$ is the actual value. Since the error terms in the equations are serially correlated as explained in the previous chapter, this

The same regression is performed on the wage change in durable-goods industries, $^d w_t$, and nondurable-goods industries, $^n w_t$, in place of all manufacturing; and now the corresponding unemployment rates in manufacturing durables, $^d U_t$, and nondurables, $^n U_t$, are used in place of the total civilian labor force unemployment rate, $U_t$, that is used in the equations for all manufacturing. The resulting estimates are

$$^d w_t = -1.573 + \underset{(10.559)}{41.583 \; ^d U_t^{-1}} - \underset{(17.434)}{49.861 \; ^d U_t^{-2}} + e_t,$$
$$R^2 = 0.419, \qquad (3.3a)$$

and

$$^n w_t = -10.184 + \underset{(29.689)}{115.772 \; ^n U_t^{-1}} - \underset{(62.534)}{210.515 \; ^n U_t^{-2}} + e_t,$$
$$R^2 = 0.341. \qquad (3.3b)$$

The considerable difference in the size of the coefficients and constant terms in these two equations is not surprising. Since the two unemployment terms have different signs, big changes in both coefficients are largely offsetting in their total effect. The lower values of $R^2$ in both these equations compared to Equation 3.3 present a more substantive difference. The regressions on $^d w_t$ and $^n w_t$ were rerun with the $^d U_t$ and $^n U_t$ variables replaced by the equivalent $U_t$ terms. The results with the broader unemployment series were better in each case. For durables, $R^2$ went from 0.419 to 0.523, while for nondurables it went from 0.341 to 0.489. This is evidence that the more aggregated series may be the appropriate one for explaining wage changes in the two manufacturing subsectors. A similar comparison is made when the fully specified model is estimated later in the chapter.

## Adding the Cost of Living

The cost of living may be brought into the explanation of money wage rates either by reducing money wages to real terms, or by introducing prices explicitly as an additional explanatory variable. The first alternative is unnecessarily restrictive and inconsistent with a model of bargaining for money wages. Furthermore, an initial

---

assumption is not quite valid; but no attempt is made to adjust for this. The ratio of a coefficient estimate to its standard error is therefore used to test the null hypothesis that the true coefficient is zero.

look at scatter diagrams of real and money wage rates plotted against unemployment suggests that the conversion to real wages is not a fruitful one. Therefore the effect of prices is brought in through an additional variable.

Two possible forms are considered for a cost-of-living variable: it may be based on (1) quarter-by-quarter adjustment of all wages to changes in living costs, designated $c_t$, or (2) the adjustment of just those wages up for annual renegotiation to changes in living costs over the past year, designated $c_t^*$. Both these forms are discussed in the sections on the model of wage determination and on the construction of data. It is appropriate here to point out that the former, $c_t$, involves price changes over a four-quarter period, contemporaneous with the period over which wage changes are measured if neither variable is lagged; while the latter involves price changes over a seven-quarter period. That is,

$$c_t = \frac{C_t - C_{t-1}}{C_{t-1}} + \frac{C_{t-1} - C_{t-2}}{C_{t-2}} + \frac{C_{t-2} - C_{t-3}}{C_{t-3}}$$
$$+ \frac{C_{t-3} - C_{t-4}}{C_{t-4}}, \quad (3.4a)$$

and

$$c_t^* = \frac{C_t - C_{t-4}}{C_{t-4}} + \frac{C_{t-1} - C_{t-5}}{C_{t-5}} + \frac{C_{t-2} - C_{t-6}}{C_{t-6}}$$
$$+ \frac{C_{t-3} - C_{t-7}}{C_{t-7}}, \quad (3.4b)$$

where $C_t$ is the level of the cost of living in the current quarter.

The results of introducing various living-cost terms into the regression are summarized in Table 3.1. The results are shown for each living-cost variable used with a one-quarter lag, indicated by $c_{t-1}$ and $c_{t-1}^*$, and as an alternative, with no lag at all. Lags of two quarters were also tried, but proved inferior to the cases shown. Some lag is preferred *a priori* since it most clearly shows the intended causality running from the cost of living to wages and allows for the expected lag in adjusting wages to living costs. This adjustment may be so rapid, however, that the unlagged form is appropriate for a quarterly model, and this is why both are shown. The table shows the fraction of variation explained by regressions using the different living-cost terms together with the explanatory variables in Equations 3.3, 3.3*a*, and 3.3*b* for the three wage-change categories: all manufacturing, durable-goods, and nondurable-goods industries.

TABLE 3.1

EFFECT OF ADDING DIFFERENT COST-OF-LIVING TERMS TO THE
EARLIER REGRESSIONS EXPLAINING WAGE CHANGES BY
UNEMPLOYMENT RATES

| Aggregation Level | Price Term Used | $R^2$ |
|---|---|---|
| All Manufacturing | none | 0.498 |
| | $c_{t-1}$ | 0.732 |
| | $c_t$ | 0.760 |
| | $\overset{*}{c}_{t-1}$ | 0.551 |
| | $\overset{*}{c}_t$ | 0.719 |
| Durable-Goods Industries | none | 0.419 |
| | $c_{t-1}$ | 0.764 |
| | $c_t$ | 0.688 |
| | $\overset{*}{c}_{t-1}$ | 0.644 |
| | $\overset{*}{c}_t$ | 0.743 |
| Nondurable-Goods Industries | none | 0.341 |
| | $c_{t-1}$ | 0.704 |
| | $c_t$ | 0.729 |
| | $\overset{*}{c}_{t-1}$ | 0.486 |
| | $\overset{*}{c}_t$ | 0.631 |

From Table 3.1, it is clear that the living-cost term without asterisk is better than the one with, and it is the variable chosen for this study. Figure 3.5 shows a graph of $c_t$ for each quarter in the postwar period covered by this study.

The choice of the lag is less clear. In nondurables and all manufacturing, the regressions with $c_t$ explain slightly more than those with $c_{t-1}$. In durables, however, $c_{t-1}$ does considerably better, giving an $R^2$ of 0.764 compared with 0.688 with $c_t$. On this basis, the preferred specification, with $c_{t-1}$, will be used for now, and $c_t$ will be held as an alternative to be tried again when other explanatory variables are added.

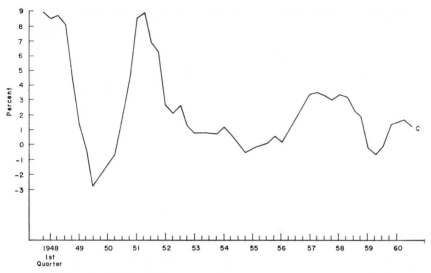

FIGURE 3.5. *Rates of change in living costs over the postwar period.* Annual percentage changes in cost of living $c$ (consumers price index), by quarters, from 1947-IV to 1960-III.

The regressions with the cost-of-living term added are now as follows:

for all manufacturing,

$$w_t = -1.445 + 31.686\, U_t^{-1} - 37.380\, U_t^{-2} + 0.466\, c_{t-1} + e_t,$$
$$(9.240) \qquad\qquad (18.547) \qquad\qquad (0.064)$$
$$R^2 = 0.732; \qquad (3.5)$$

for durables,

$$^d w_t = -1.429 + 11.490\, {}^d U_t^{-1} - 6.733\, {}^d U_t^{-2} + 0.560\, c_{t-1} + e_t,$$
$$(7.731) \qquad\qquad (12.405) \qquad\qquad (0.068)$$
$$R^2 = 0.764; \qquad (3.5a)$$

and for nondurables,

$$^n w_t = -0.830 + 27.792\, {}^n U_t^{-1} - 39.083\, {}^n U_t^{-2} + 0.531\, c_{t-1} + e_t,$$
$$(23.298) \qquad\qquad (48.168) \qquad\qquad (0.071)$$
$$R^2 = 0.704. \qquad (3.5b)$$

Adding the cost-of-living term improves the explanatory power of all equations a great deal. For all manufacturing, the $R^2$ is raised from 0.498 to 0.732; for durable-goods industries, the change is from 0.419 to 0.764; and for nondurables it is from 0.341 to 0.704.

## Some Implications of the Preliminary Wage Equation

Before going further, it is useful here to examine some of the properties of the estimates using just unemployment and price changes. Although the argument of this study involves additional explanatory variables, others have discussed models using just these two, and some comparisons are in order. Since most comments apply to all the equations estimated, unless otherwise stated reference will be to the equation for all manufacturing to avoid needless repetition.

The first point to observe is that the form of the equation gives a rather unexpected curve relating unemployment and wage changes. In a relation such as $w_t = a_0 + a_1 U_t^{-1} + a_2 U_t^{-2}$, both $a_1$ and $a_2$ must be positive for a curve relating $w_t$ and $U_t$ to slope downward and be concave from above for all values of $U_t$. The estimates for $a_2$ in all the preceding equations are negative. The curve associated with these estimates rises for low values of $U_t$, then turns and takes on the expected shape, having a negative slope, and shortly afterward becoming concave from above for all higher values of $U_t$. The turning point beyond which the slope of the curve is negative can be calculated from the coefficients of the unemployment terms. For Equation 3.5, this point comes at $U_t$ equals 2.36; for 3.5a, at $^d U_t$ equals 1.16; and for 3.5b, at $^n U_t$ equals 2.78. In the present arrangement of the data, no observations are recorded to the left of these turning points. Since the perverse shape, the positive slope, occurs outside the area of observed values of $U_t$, it has no predictive significance in this range. It is of interest, however, that no observations were recorded that forced the curve to approach the $w_t$ axis asymptotically. If in the range of experience covered by the data, low unemployment were associated with very sharp wage increases, the curve would have been forced to slope steeply upward as it approached the $w_t$ axis. That this did not occur is some evidence that the labor markets of the economy do not work this way. It raises the possibility that the institutional environment associated with American wage bargaining acts to modify extreme wage increases in times of tight labor markets. And this is an interesting possible corollary to the proposition often put forth that the wage-setting institutions are inflationary because they keep wages rising in times of excess labor supplies.

## Inflation and the Preliminary Wage Equation

The conditions for wage and price stability implied by the regression equations could be computed. But wage stability is an unreasonable goal in an economy with rising labor productivity unless full downward flexibility of prices is assumed.[2] And wage and price stability together would have all the benefits of productivity increases that accrue to profits. More interesting and important are the conditions for price stability that can be inferred from the wage equation and some assumptions about the relation between wages, productivity, and prices.

The productivity statistic relevant for this purpose is the change in aggregate labor productivity adjusted to remove the effect of relative interindustry shifts in output. If wage rates (including fringes) everywhere rise at the same rate as this average productivity, an aggregate price index can remain stable while the relative shares of wage and nonwage incomes remain unchanged. In addition, if prices in individual industries change in relation to the difference between productivity gains in each industry and the rate of wage change, relative shares in each industry will remain unchanged. These observations suggest the neutral standard that wage changes are noninflationary if they proceed at a rate equal to the rate of aggregate productivity gains. And consistent with this, the estimated wage equations will be analyzed on the assumption that living costs change by the difference between rates of wage change and rates of aggregate productivity increase.

Since this study is limited to the manufacturing sector, applying this rule to manufacturing wages implies manufacturing prices will change relative to living costs to the extent manufacturing productivity gains differ from the economy average. Finally, it should be emphasized that unless wage costs are the sole determinants of prices, the rule just outlined for linking wages to inflation cannot tell what will actually happen to prices, only what is consistent with a reasonable neutral standard for price behavior.

If 2.5 percent per year is assumed to be the average growth in hourly labor productivity, the unemployment rate implied by Equation 3.5 to keep wages rising at this same rate is 6.6 percent. With a more optimistic rate of productivity increase of 3.0 percent, the unemployment implied for this rate of wage increase is 5.6 percent.[3] Both these are stable price solutions.

[2] According to Equation 3.5, an unemployment rate just over 20 percent is needed to keep wages stable with stable living costs.

[3] Asking the same question of the equations estimated for the two manufacturing subsectors, Equations 3.5a and 3.5b, shows that for wage increases of 3 percent annually, unemployment in durable-goods industries would have to be 6.7 percent, while unemployment in nondurables would have to be 5.3 percent.

More generally, Equation 3.5 can be solved for the relation between wage changes and unemployment for rates of price change
other than zero. Computing the price change according to the productivity rule and feeding it back into the wage equation yields

$$w_t = -2.71 + 59.3\, U_t^{-1} - 70.0\, U_t^{-2} - 0.872\rho_t \qquad (3.5c)$$

as the steady state solution for $w_t$, where $\rho_t$ is the aggregate rate of
productivity change excluding interindustry shift effects. Figure 3.6

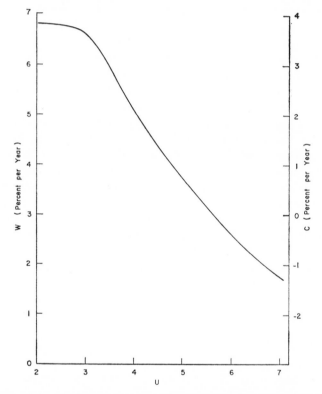

FIGURE 3.6.  *Preliminary wage change-unemployment-inflation relation.*
Preliminary wage change-unemployment-inflation relation (from Equation 3.5, on the assumption that percentage changes in living costs *c*
proceed at a rate 3 percentage points less than wage change *w*).

plots this relation for $\rho_t$ equal to 3 percent per year. That figure
shows that steady 4 percent unemployment would involve a 5.2

percent rate of wage increase and 2.2 percent annual rate of inflation.

These results are at best only suggestive at this point. The best guess regarding these and other questions must be postponed until the wage equation is more fully specified. However, the present results can be compared with those of the British studies which used no more than these explanatory variables. Phillips found for his long-term relation for Britain that an unemployment rate of 2.5 percent would be consistent with wages rising no faster than 2 percent per year.[4] And using Lipsey's estimated relation,[5] unemployment of 5.6 percent in Britain would be associated with wage increases of less than 1 percent per year, compared with 3 percent for the stable price case in this study's estimate for the United States. Unfortunately, such comparisons are elusive because of the differences in measuring unemployment in the two countries. Some recent studies suggest that the British statistic should be increased by roughly 50 percent to make it comparable with the American definition.[6] This still leaves the American figures substantially higher.

The coefficient for cost-of-living changes gives another basis for comparing the two countries, and here there is no significant problem of dissimilar measurements. The coefficient for $c_{t-1}$ in the all-manufacturing equation of this study is 0.466. This is somewhat lower than Lipsey's coefficient of 0.69, which he however revises in a footnote to between 0.4 and 0.5,[7] and virtually the same as the estimate by Dicks-Mireaux and Dow[8] of 0.5. It is decidedly below the estimate of 0.98 in the study by Klein and Ball.[9] However, this last estimate is suspect as explained in Chapter 1. Taking a consensus of the three sources of estimates for Britain, the present estimate of the price coefficient for America is lower or perhaps the same.

[4] Phillips, A. W., "The Relationship Between Unemployment and the Rate of Change of Money Wage Rates in the United Kingdom, 1861–1957," *Economica*, N.S. 25 (November 1958), p. 299.

[5] Lipsey, Richard G., "The Relationship Between Unemployment and the Rate of Change of Money Wage Rates in the United Kingdom, 1862–1957: A Further Analysis," *Economica*, N.S. 27 (February 1960), p. 26.

[6] See, for example, Appendix A in *Measuring Employment and Unemployment* by the President's Committee to Appraise Employment and Unemployment Statistics (Washington, D. C.: U.S. Government Printing Office, 1962).

[7] *Ibid.*, p. 25.

[8] Dicks-Mireaux, L. A., and J. C. R. Dow, "The Determinants of Wage Inflation: The United Kingdom, 1946–1956," *The Journal of the Royal Statistical Society*, Series A, 22(2) (1959).

[9] Klein, L. R., and R. J. Ball, "Some Econometrics of Determination of Absolute Prices and Wages," *Economic Journal*, Vol. 69 (September 1959).

### Profit Rates and the Full Model of Wage Determination

*Profit Rates*

The next important variable in the present model of wage determination is the profit rate, defined as earnings after taxes divided by stockholders' equity. The average annual profit rate over the past four quarters is used for this study. Quarterly series on this variable were prepared for all manufacturing and for the durable-goods and nondurable-goods subsectors and are designated as $R_t$, $^dR_t$, and $^nR_t$ respectively. Figure 3.7 is a graph of $R_t$ plotted for each quarter covered by the study. In adding profit rate to the regression, the unemployment effect is streamlined by using only one term, $U_t^{-1}$, to reflect it. With both $U_t^{-1}$ and $U_t^{-2}$ in the equation, the standard

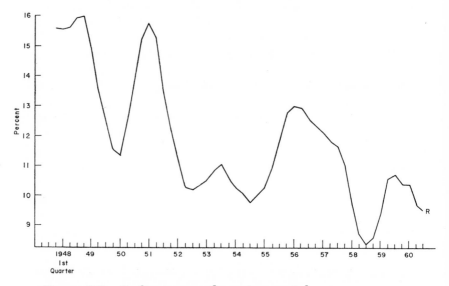

FIGURE 3.7.  *Profit rates over the postwar period.*
Index of average profit rate after taxes over last four quarters for all
manufacturing corporations, $R$, by quarters from 1947-IV to 1960-III.

error of the coefficients of each term becomes large. This means close bounds cannot be placed on the actual value of the coefficients. In the case of the durable-goods and nondurable-goods subgroups, this problem was already evident in Equations 3.5*a* and 3.5*b*. The problem is an outcome of the high correlation between $U_t^{-1}$ and $U_t^{-2}$ rather than an indication of the relevance of unemployment in the explanation of wage changes. Using only $U_t^{-1}$

still maintains the nonlinear form of the unemployment-wage relation and sharpens the estimate of the unemployment term. It allows the use of ready tests of statistical significance and of the relative importance of unemployment compared to the other variables. On the other hand, there is some loss of flexibility in fitting the unemployment relation with only one term, and final results later in the chapter will be checked again using both.

The regressions, using profit rates and cost of living lagged one quarter together with a single variable for unemployment, are as follows:

for all manufacturing,

$$w_t = -\,3.831 + \underset{(0.063)}{0.312}\,c_{t-1} + \underset{(2.597)}{13.525}\,U_t{}^{-1} + \underset{(0.081)}{0.404}\,R_{t-1} + e_t,$$

$$R^2 = 0.810; \qquad (3.6)$$

for the durable-goods subsector,

$$^dw_t = -\,0.572 + \underset{(0.061)}{0.497}\,c_{t-1} + \underset{(1.492)}{6.702}\,{}^dU_t{}^{-1} + \underset{(0.052)}{0.228}\,{}^dR_{t-1} + e_t,$$

$$R^2 = 0.806; \qquad (3.6a)$$

and for the nondurable-goods subsector,

$$^nw_t = -\,4.774 + \underset{(0.059)}{0.288}\,c_{t-1} + \underset{(2.387)}{11.962}\,{}^nU_t{}^{-1} + \underset{(0.076)}{0.516}\,{}^nR_{t-1} + e_t,$$

$$R^2 = 0.853. \qquad (3.6b)$$

These results strongly support a theory of wage determination calling for the simultaneous inclusion of all three of the explanatory variables. In each regression, the coefficient estimates have the sign expected according to the theory outlined in Chapter 2. Furthermore, the estimates are easily significant at the 0.99 confidence level, each coefficient being more than three times its standard error.

## Variables of Change

Most of the recent work done on the question of an equation for wage determination in the economy has specifically included a dynamic explanatory variable of either profits or unemployment. Similarly, in the present study reasons were given for expecting such a variable to play a role in explaining wage behavior. It was further argued that either a variable for the change in profits or the change in unemployment would serve the same purpose since the basis for their inclusion is to account for expectations that could be measured by either. Accordingly, series were constructed to measure both changes in profit rates and in unemployment.

For unemployment, two dummy variables, $^RD_t$ and $^FD_t$, were constructed to indicate persistent periods of either rising or falling unemployment, since the significant movements of unemployment are the contraction and expansion phases of major business cycles. These variables had the value one or zero before aggregation over four-quarter intervals, depending on whether unemployment was rising or falling, and both had value zero during periods when unemployment was not moving significantly in either direction. To measure changes in profit rate, the first differences of the profit-rate series were used.[10]

Several regressions were run for all manufacturing to determine the effect of the dynamic variables. The result of introducing the unemployment-change terms $^RD_t$ and $^FD_t$ is as follows:

$$w_t = -3.334 + \underset{(0.058)}{0.294\,c_{t-1}} + \underset{(3.035)}{13.355\,U_t{}^{-1}} + \underset{(0.076)}{0.376\,R_{t-1}}$$

$$-\underset{(0.578)}{1.123\,{}^RD_t} + \underset{(0.518)}{0.859\,{}^FD_t} + e_t, \qquad R^2 = 0.854. \qquad (3.7)$$

Two observations are interesting. One is that the other coefficient estimates are virtually unchanged by the introduction of the new terms. The other is that the new terms raise the percentage of variation explained from 0.810 to 0.854.

Using the change in profit rate $\Delta R_t$ instead of the unemployment-change terms gives even better results. The estimated multiple regression equation is now

$$w_t = -4.313 + \underset{(0.054)}{0.367\,c_{t-1}} + \underset{(2.188)}{14.711\,U_t{}^{-1}}$$

$$+ \underset{(0.068)}{0.424\,R_{t-1}} + \underset{(0.176)}{0.796\,\Delta R_t} + e_t, \qquad R^2 = 0.870. \qquad (3.8)$$

The percentage of variation explained is somewhat higher than in Equation 3.7. Again the changes in the other coefficient estimates are slight, although now all three are increased rather than de-

---

[10] Since profit rate is an inherently trendless variable, it is not necessary to use percentage changes as it is with variables such as wages and prices. The simple difference is also more convenient for later use.

creased. All coefficients are easily significant at the 0.99 probability level.

Finally, using both the change in profit rate and direction of unemployment terms together gives the following equation:

$$w_t = -2.873 + \underset{(0.057)}{0.346} c_{t-1} + \underset{(2.805)}{13.192} U_t{}^{-1} + \underset{(0.072)}{0.428} R_{t-1}$$
$$+ \underset{(0.244)}{0.700} \Delta R_t - \underset{(0.585)}{0.423} {}^R D_t$$
$$+ \underset{(0.560)}{0.006} {}^F D_t + e_t, \qquad R^2 = 0.879. \qquad (3.9)$$

This result confirms the comparison of the two previous equations favoring $\Delta R_t$ as an explanatory variable. In Equation 3.9, the coefficients of the direction of unemployment terms are not significant,[11] and more important, the direction of unemployment terms add almost nothing to the explanation obtained from the change in profits term alone.

To summarize, it appears that a variable expressing changes in economic conditions is significant in explaining wage behavior, and the change in profit rate is a better variable for this purpose than the direction in which unemployment is moving. Equation 3.8 is thus the preferred equation embodying all the aspects of the wage-determination model that were outlined in the previous chapter.

Introducing variables for the change in profits in durable-goods and nondurable-goods industries into the equations explaining wage changes in these subgroups gave the following estimates:

for durables,

$$^d w_t = -0.767 + \underset{(0.058)}{0.532} c_{t-1} + \underset{(1.382)}{7.166} {}^d U_t{}^{-1}$$
$$+ \underset{(0.064)}{0.240} {}^d R_{t-1} + \underset{(0.160)}{0.488} {}^d \Delta R_t + e_t, \qquad R^2 = 0.839; \qquad (3.8a)$$

and for nondurables,

$$^n w_t = -5.230 + \underset{(0.054)}{0.313} c_{t-1} + \underset{(2.170)}{12.458} {}^n U_t{}^{-1}$$
$$+ \underset{(0.068)}{0.548} {}^n R_{t-1} + \underset{(0.180)}{0.592} {}^n \Delta R_t + e_t, \qquad R^2 = 0.882. \qquad (3.8b)$$

[11] Actually, a significance test from the standard errors is not a fair one for comparison since there are two dummy variables for unemployment. However, at least the second term, $^F D$, is insignificantly different from zero by any standard.

The results of adding the last variable are similar in both cases to the result for all manufacturing: the other coefficients do not change much; the $R^2$ rises appreciably, from 0.81 to 0.84 for durables and from 0.85 to 0.88 for nondurables; and all coefficient estimates have the expected sign and are highly significant.

The squared partial correlation coefficients of wage changes with each dependent variable further illustrate the case for including all four explanatory variables in the regression on wage changes. These coefficients, together with the simple (total) squared correlations between wage changes and each dependent variable are given in Table 3.2 for each industry subgroup and for all manufacturing.

TABLE 3.2

PARTIAL AND TOTAL SQUARED CORRELATION COEFFICIENTS OF VARIABLES IN FINAL WAGE EQUATIONS 3.8, 3.8$a$, AND 3.8$b$

| Squared Partial Correlation Coefficients | | | |
|---|---|---|---|
| Aggregation Level* | $w_t c_{t-1}$ | $w_t U_t{}^{-1}$ | $w_t R_{t-1}$ | $w_t \Delta R_t$ |
| All Manufacturing | 0.508 | 0.501 | 0.456 | 0.316 |
| Durable-Goods Industries | 0.654 | 0.375 | 0.219 | 0.171 |
| Nondurable-Goods Industries | 0.430 | 0.423 | 0.590 | 0.194 |

| Squared Simple (Total) Correlation Coefficients | | | |
|---|---|---|---|
| Aggregation Level* | $w_t c_{t-1}$ | $w_t R_{t-1}$ | $w_t R_{t-1}$ | $w_t \Delta R_t$ |
| All Manufacturing | 0.585 | 0.381 | 0.503 | 0.009(−) |
| Durable-Goods Industries | 0.658 | 0.318 | 0.350 | 0.008(−) |
| Nondurable-Goods Industries | 0.651 | 0.182 | 0.624 | 0.017(−) |

* Variables refer to those associated with each level of aggregation, except for total manufacturing where civilian labor force unemployment rates were used.

All the variables have a significant independent effect in explaining wage changes, although their strength in this respect varies. The dynamic variable, $\Delta R_t$, is the weakest of the four in each of the three regressions. Even so, it explains 32 percent of the variance in $w_t$ remaining after taking account of the three other variables in that regression, and 19 percent and 17 percent of the remaining variance in $^n w_t$ and $^d w_t$ respectively.

Finally, the presence of first-order serial correlation in the residuals is evident in this fully specified form of the wage model. The Durbin-Watson statistic for Equation 3.8 is 1.2. As explained earlier, this is to be expected from the overlap in the independent variables that results from explaining wage changes over a one-year interval. The Durbin-Watson statistic for Equation 3.8 is nonetheless higher than it was for the estimated equations presented earlier with the incompletely specified model.

## Some Possible Alternatives to the Basic Model

Within the general specification of the model embodied in Equation 3.8, some variations are worth exploring. These include trying different lag structures for the explanatory variables and testing some alternative forms of the unemployment-rate variable.

### The Industry Subgroups

There is the possibility that part of the difference in the coefficients of unemployment for all manufacturing and the two industry subgroups results from using different series for this variable in each subgroup when in fact a single, aggregate series is appropriate. In particular, the durable-goods unemployment series has much wider swings than that for the civilian labor force as a whole. Since labor markets are not necessarily defined along industry lines, the wide swings of the unemployment series for durable goods may overstate the true variations in the pressure of unemployment on the labor markets for durable-goods industries. A better measure of these pressures may be the series of aggregate unemployment. To test this possibility the regressions for the durable and nondurable subgroups were rerun substituting the aggregate unemployment measure for that of each subgroup. The results were

$$^{d}w_t = -2.175 + \underset{(0.056)}{0.509}\, c_{t-1} + \underset{(2.519)}{14.635}\, U_t{}^{-1}$$

$$+ \underset{(0.064)}{0.224}\, {}^{d}R_{t-1} + \underset{(0.152)}{0.516}\, {}^{d}\Delta R_t + e_t, \qquad R^2 = 0.853, \qquad (3.8c)$$

and

$$^{n}w_t = -4.507 + \underset{(0.054)}{0.317}\, c_{t-1} + \underset{(2.170)}{10.343}\, U_t{}^{-1}$$

$$+ \underset{(0.068)}{0.512}\, {}^{n}R_{t-1} + \underset{(0.180)}{0.672}\, {}^{n}\Delta R_t + e_t, \qquad R^2 = 0.862. \qquad (3.8d)$$

The only big change compared to Equations 3.8a and 3.8b was in the unemployment coefficient in each equation. For durables it rose from 7.166 to 14.635, while for nondurables it fell from 12.458 to 10.343. The $R^2$ for durables increased from 0.839 to 0.853, while for nondurables it fell from 0.882 to 0.862. The relative independent importance of each variable, as measured by its squared partial correlation coefficient, was unchanged within each equation. However, the absolute value of this coefficient for the unemployment variable increased in durables from 0.375 to 0.429 and decreased in nondurables from 0.423 to 0.327. These rather mixed results for the two subgroups make any conclusions about the correct level of aggregation for the unemployment variable highly speculative. The improvement in the equation for durables, however, does show that the less volatile series works better there. It is hard to say whether this is because the different level of aggregation is more nearly the correct one, or simply because a more damped series works better as a purely analytic matter. However, in view of the conceptual difficulties of specifying an unemployment rate for a particular industry group, the equations using the aggregate unemployment statistic are probably preferable.

### Measuring "Excess" Rather than Total Unemployment

Since there is some positive level of unemployment that represents an irreducible minimum, it may be that the impact of unemployment on wages is best measured by deviations from this minimum level rather than from zero. For the purpose of testing this possibility, four different levels of unemployment were tried as minimums: 1.0, 1.5, 2.0, and 2.5 percent. For each of these, a new unemployment variable was constructed by subtracting the minimum level from the recorded unemployment. The new variables are designated $^1U_t$, $^2U_t$, $^3U_t$, and $^4U_t$, where $^1U_t$ equals $U_t - 1.0$, $^2U_t$ equals $U_t - 1.5$, and so forth. These calculations were made only for the aggregate unemployment series (civilian labor force).

The new unemployment variables were introduced into regressions of the form of Equation 3.8 to compare their explanatory power with that of the original unemployment variable. The results are summarized in Table 3.3. When the percentage of variation explained by the regression is the criterion, there is virtually no differ-

TABLE 3.3
DIFFERENT UNEMPLOYMENT TERMS IN REGRESSION ON ALL
MANUFACTURING WAGES

| Explanatory Variables | $R^2$ |
|---|---|
| $c_{t-1}$, $U_t{}^{-1}$, $R_{t-1}$, $\Delta R_t$ | 0.870 |
| $c_{t-1}$, $^1U_t{}^{-1}$, $R_{t-1}$, $\Delta R_t$ | 0.871 |
| $c_{t-1}$, $^2U_t{}^{-1}$, $R_{t-1}$, $\Delta R_t$ | 0.871 |
| $c_{t-1}$, $^3U_t{}^{-1}$, $R_{t-1}$, $\Delta R_t$ | 0.873 |
| $c_{t-1}$, $^4U_t{}^{-1}$, $R_{t-1}$, $\Delta R_t$ | 0.866 |

ence among the five forms of the unemployment variable. What difference there is suggests that the $^3U_t$ variable is best, which means the unemployment rate in excess of 2 percent is what affects the labor market. The coefficient estimates on the other explanatory variables change very little with the different unemployment variables. Thus, although there is some suggestion that a structural minimum around 2 percent should be the base against which the impact of actual unemployment rates is measured, the evidence is slight, and estimates using Equation 3.8 will yield virtually identical results.[12]

## Alternative Forms of the Unemployment Rate Variable

Next we can consider two alternative forms of the unemployment rate variable. The basic equation, 3.8, uses $U_t^{-1}$ to describe a nonlinear form for the relation of unemployment rates to wage changes. It remains to be seen whether a more general nonlinear form, using both $U_t^{-1}$ and $U_t^{-2}$ as explanatory variables in the fully specified model, results in a substantial improvement and whether a linear unemployment-rate term, simply $U_t$, is inferior to these alternatives once the effects of the other explanatory variables in the model are included. The equations fitted with these alternatives came out as follows:

$$w_t = -4.588 + \underset{(0.054)}{0.368\, c_{t-1}} + \underset{(6.858)}{18.279\, U_t^{-1}}$$

$$-\underset{(13.875)}{7.624\, U_t^{-2}} + \underset{(0.072)}{0.412\, R_{t-1}}$$

$$+ \underset{(0.180)}{0.776\, \Delta R_t} + e_t, \qquad R^2 = 0.871; \qquad (3.10)$$

$$w_t = 3.287 + \underset{(0.061)}{0.375\, c_{t-1}} - \underset{(0.162)}{0.769\, U_t}$$

$$+ \underset{(0.072)}{0.368\, R_{t-1}} + \underset{(0.182)}{0.828\, \Delta R_t} + e_t, \qquad R^2 = 0.859. \qquad (3.11)$$

From these results, the basic equation, 3.8, remains the preferred one. The earlier preference for the nonlinear unemployment relation

---

[12] Interestingly, in a different context, N. J. Simler has estimated a 2 percent structural minimum for the unemployment rate. See his "Long-term Unemployment, the Structural Hypothesis, and Public Policy," *American Economic Review*, Vol. 54 (December 1964).

is strengthened by the somewhat smaller $R^2$ of Equation 3.11 compared with 3.8. And the difference between Equations 3.8 and 3.10 is insignificant, both in explanatory power and in the estimates of wage change that would result from any set of values for the explanatory variables within the range of our postwar experience.

*An Unlagged Variation*

Although specification of the lags between variables in the relation to be tested is necessary and useful, it is worthwhile to test reasonable alternatives also. In particular, the effect of removing all the lags from the dependent variables is an important case to examine. Since most of the variables used are significantly correlated with one another, it is possible that specifying lags in some would influence measures of their relative importance. Fitting the original equations with all lags dropped from the dependent variables gives the following results:[13]

for all manufacturing,

$$w_t = -\ 4.562 +\ \underset{(0.057)}{0.342}\ c_t + \underset{(2.277)}{16.045}\ U_t{}^{-1} + \underset{(0.076)}{0.424}\ R_t$$
$$+\ \underset{(0.180)}{0.048}\ \Delta R_t + e_t, \qquad R^2 = 0.854; \qquad (3.12)$$

for durable goods,

$$^dw_t = 0.979 +\ \underset{(0.077)}{0.446}\ c_t + \underset{(1.761)}{8.113}\ {}^dU_t{}^{-1} + \underset{(0.088)}{0.252}\ {}^dR_t$$
$$-\ \underset{(0.222)}{0.048}\ {}^d\Delta R_t + e_t, \qquad R^2 = 0.735; \qquad (3.12a)$$

and for nondurable goods,

$$^nw_t = -\ 5.115 +\ \underset{(0.050)}{0.340}\ c_t + \underset{(2.043)}{12.936}\ {}^nU_t{}^{-1} + \underset{(0.064)}{0.524}\ {}^nR_t$$
$$-\ \underset{(0.164)}{0.384}\ {}^n\Delta R_t + e_t, \qquad R^2 = 0.892. \qquad (3.12b)$$

The original form of Equations 3.8 and 3.8*a,b* seems preferable to these. The only large change in the fraction of variation explained

---

[13] The problem of biased estimates arising in single-equation estimation when the equation is in fact part of a nonrecursive system appears most prominent in regressions on all unlagged variables such as these. This problem is dealt with in Chapter 5. As mentioned earlier, we can anticipate the results of that chapter by saying that all conclusions reached now with the simple least-squares estimates are validated there.

is in the durable-goods equation where the original form had $R^2$ equal to 0.839 compared with only 0.735 in the present unlagged version. In all three of the present equations, the term for change in profits has become insignificant or has the wrong sign. In other respects, the two forms are similar; and it is interesting that the elasticity of wages to living costs actually declines a bit. With no empirical evidence favoring the unlagged alternative, and with some evidence even arguing against it, the preferred form remains the original one.

## Major Implications of the Wage Equation

It is now time to examine some implications of the wage equation developed in this chapter. Of primary interest is the trade-off between wage changes and the explanatory variables, especially unemployment. With the complete formulation of the wage equation given by Equation 3.8, we are now in a position to examine the wage change-unemployment relationship in a more realistic framework than was afforded by a regression between just these two variables. Since the present hypothesis on wage determination calls for the simultaneous interaction of several variables to explain wage changes, the basic wage change-unemployment relation must be viewed with all these variables accounted for. The previous calculations on this point must be considered as preliminary, although they served the purpose of allowing comparisons between the American experience recorded in this study and that of Great Britain as recorded by other authors. The relations reported by others, such as the original Phillips' curve[14] and the sketch of a relation by Samuelson and Solow for the United States,[15] must also be considered preliminary if the model of this study has any general applicability.

Of course, the present discussion is hardly the last word itself. Different, and particularly more disaggregated, approaches may reveal refinements or qualifications to the results. The present study is based on the belief that aggregate relationships exist. The empirical results of this chapter support this belief, but do not rule out the possibility of fruitful study at other levels. Also, the analysis of an equation such as 3.8 can be augmented with more dynamic

[14] Phillips, *op. cit.*

[15] Samuelson, Paul A., and Robert Solow, "Analytical Aspect of Anti-inflation Policy," *Papers and Proceedings of the American Economic Association,* Vol. 50 (May 1960), pp. 187–189.

analysis involving a more detailed look at the feedback of wage changes onto other economic variables. Among other things, this would answer the question of whether the wage-price relations form a convergent system which is necessary if the steady state, limit calculations made here are to have relevance. But such considerations will be postponed until Chapter 5.

### Noninflationary Wage Changes

The first question asked of Equation 3.8 is the following: What constant level of unemployment is consistent with wage changes such that the cost of living, profit rate, and the relative shares of profits and wages all remain constant?[16] The answer will depend on the rate of increase of average labor productivity (adjusted, as before, to remove interindustry shift effects) as well as on the level of profit rates.[17] Solving Equation 3.8 for $U_t$, with $c_{t-1}$ and $\Delta R_t$ equal to zero, yields

$$U_t = \frac{14.711}{4.313 + w_t - 0.424\,R_{t-1}}. \tag{3.13}$$

For specified rates of profit, this equation gives the relation between $U_t$ and $w_t$ on the assumption that $w_t$ corresponds to the adjusted rate of productivity increase, $\rho_t$. The condition that the Consumer Price Index will not rise at all is probably too severe, even for the problem of noninflationary wage changes. It is frequently said that this and other price indexes fail to account fully for quality improvements and are thus biased upward. If such a bias is continuing and constant, in the sense that actual productivity gains are continually more rapid than recorded and true rates of price increase are slower, then zero true inflation would correspond to some steady rate of increase in published price indexes. This condition would not affect the estimation that has been done here, only the absolute standard that is appropriate in interpreting the results. Further on, calculations are made in which some inflation in the published indexes is permitted, and these may represent a more realistic target for policy.

[16] There is no contradiction in requiring that wages change while the profit rate and relative shares stay constant. All that is necessary is that equity grow at the same rate as the wage bill and profits.

[17] Again here and in what follows, wages and prices in other sectors of the economy are assumed to behave in a way consistent with what has been estimated here for manufacturing. This and the other assumptions implicit in this treatment were discussed earlier in connection with the preliminary wage equation.

The average value of $R_{t-1}$ over the 1947–1960 period was 11.8. When this value is used in Equation 3.13, the unemployment levels associated with 2.5, 3.0, 3.5, and 4.0 percent per year wage increases are as shown in the first part of Table 3.4.

TABLE 3.4

RELATION OF WAGE CHANGE TO UNEMPLOYMENT
FOR DIFFERENT PROFIT RATES

(from Equation 3.8 with $c_{t-1} = \Delta R_t = 0$, and productivity
assumed to grow at the rate $w_t$)

| | $w_t$ (present increase per year) | $U_t$ (percent) |
|---|---|---|
| For $R_{t-1} = 11.8$ (1947–1960 average) | 2.5 | 8.1 |
| | 3.0 | 6.4 |
| | 3.5 | 5.2 |
| | 4.0 | 4.4 |
| For $R_{t-1} = 10.8$ (1953–1960 average) | 2.5 | 6.6 |
| | 3.0 | 5.4 |
| | 3.5 | 4.5 |
| | 4.0 | 3.9 |
| For $R_{t-1} = 10.0$ | 2.5 | 5.7 |
| | 3.0 | 4.8 |
| | 3.5 | 4.1 |
| | 4.0 | 3.6 |

These results offer little hope of combining low unemployment rates with complete stability in average prices. With adjusted hourly productivity growing at a 3.0 percent annual rate, probably the best guess of what is likely to happen, price stability implies a needed unemployment rate of 6.4 percent with profit rates at their 1947–1960 average. And with this profit rate, even what appears to be a grossly optimistic rate of aggregate productivity growth of 4.0 percent requires a 4.4 percent unemployment rate for price stability.

The unemployment condition improves considerably if other profit-rate levels are assumed. The 1947–1960 period includes the immediate postwar years when profit rates were well above average. An obvious alternative is the post-Korean period, 1953–1960, when profit rates averaged 10.8 percent.

Using this, the second part of Table 3.4 shows that an unemployment rate of 5.4 percent is associated with 3.0 percent wage and

productivity increases. And with a 10.0 percent profit rate, the same
conditions imply a 4.8 percent unemployment rate. While changing
profit rates thus offer sharp improvements in the unemployment-
inflation trade-off, even the lowest rate considered here is not promising for the compatibility of stable prices and low unemployment.
Even with profit rates at 10.0 percent and a 3.5 percent rate of productivity gain, the associated unemployment rate is still just above
4.0 percent. And recent experience suggests profit rates will not
stay nearly this low.

TABLE 3.5

RELATION OF WAGE CHANGE TO UNEMPLOYMENT FROM
ALTERNATIVE WAGE EQUATIONS

(Equations 3.11, 3.10, and 3.8 with $R_{t-1} = 10.8$,
$c_{t-1} = 0$, $\Delta R_t = 0$)

|  | $w_t$ (present increase per year) | $U_t$ (percent) |
|---|---|---|
| Equation 3.11 | 2.5 | 6.2 |
| ($U_t$) | 3.0 | 5.5 |
|  | 3.5 | 4.9 |
|  | 4.0 | 4.2 |
| Equation 3.10 | 2.5 | 6.4 |
| ($U_t^{-1}, U_t^{-2}$) | 3.0 | 5.3 |
|  | 3.5 | 4.5 |
|  | 4.0 | 3.9 |
| Equation 3.8 | 2.5 | 6.6 |
| ($U_t^{-1}$) | 3.0 | 5.4 |
|  | 3.5 | 4.5 |
|  | 4.0 | 3.9 |

These conclusions are not narrowly specific to the particular form
of the wage relation represented by Equation 3.8. Table 3.5 shows
the same relationship, calculated from the alternative Equations 3.10
and 3.11, for the middle value of profit rate, 10.8 percent. The calculations from Table 3.4 (Equation 3.8) are also given here for ease in
comparing the three equations. All yield similar quantitative estimates of the required unemployment rates.

All the calculations made above serve to confirm one qualitative
point: the evidence is that the economy that generated Equation
3.8 will not operate at low unemployment rates without an inflationary rate of wage increase, at least as recorded by current price
indexes. Without significant institutional or structural changes, full

employment and complete price-index stability are incompatible goals.

## Inflation and Unemployment

Although *complete* price stability imposes excessive costs in terms of unemployment, it appears that reasonably low unemployment rates could be maintained without leading to *exceptional* rates of inflation. The rate of price increase associated with different unemployment rates depends on the prevailing profit rate and rate of productivity increase. As before, productivity can be used to relate wage and price changes in order to solve prices out of Equation 3.8. The resulting wage relation for the steady-state case is

$$w_t = -\,6.814 - 0.5797\,\rho_t + 23.24\,U_t{}^{-1} + 0.670\,R_t; \tag{3.14}$$

while the parallel equation for computing rates of price increase directly is

$$c_t = -\,6.814 - 1.5797\,\rho_t + 23.24\,U_t{}^{-1} + 0.670\,R_t. \tag{3.15}$$

In Figure 3.8a, productivity growth is assumed to proceed at a 2.7 percent annual rate, and the relations between rates of wage and price change and rates of unemployment are plotted for each of four profit rates: 12.5 percent, 11.8 percent (the 1947–1960 average), 10.8 percent (the 1953–1960 average), and 10.0 percent. Figures 3.8b, 3.8c, and 3.8d plot the same information for assumed rates of productivity growth of 3.0 percent, 3.3 percent, and 3.6 percent.

One point that is clearly illustrated by the graphs is the increasingly steep trade-off between inflation and unemployment as lower unemployment rates are reached. The difference in the rate of inflation implied for an economy at 4.0 percent rather than 5.0 percent unemployment, with the same profit rates prevailing in each case, is a little over 1 percentage point per year. However, for still lower unemployment rates, the trade-off becomes more severe due to the nonlinear form estimated for the unemployment relation. Between a steady 4.0 percent unemployment rate and one of 3.0 percent, there is about a 2 percentage point difference in the associated rate of inflation, again with the same profit rates prevailing.

The impact of more rapid rates of productivity growth can be seen in moving from one graph to the next. For instance, on the assumption that profit rates stay at 10.8 percent, 4.0 percent unemployment is associated with roughly 2.0 percent, 1.5 percent, 1.0

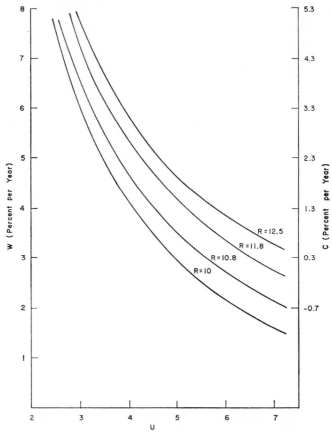

FIGURE 3.8a. *Final wage change-unemployment-inflation relation* (from Equation 3.8, for each of four profit rates R), with productivity growing at 2.7 percent annually.

percent, and 0.5 percent rates of inflation in the four graphs. Thus a reduction of 0.5 percent in the annual rate of inflation is associated with each increment of 0.3 percent in the rate of productivity gain. However, it should be emphasized that these calculations assume profit rates are the same in each case. Alternative assumptions could also be read from the graphs.

Reading across a horizontal line in any figure illustrates the impact of varying profit rates. For instance, with profit rates at 12.5 percent rather than 10.8 percent, the same inflation rates are now associated with about 5.0 percent unemployment rather than 4.0 percent.

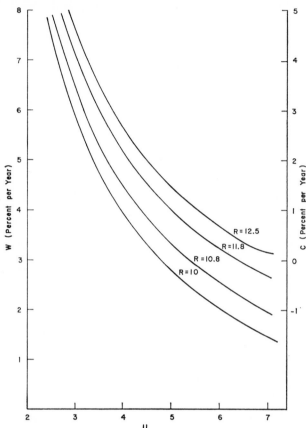

FIGURE 3.8b.  *Final wage change-unemployment-inflation relation* (from Equation 3.8, for each of four profit rates R), with productivity growing at 3 percent annually.

These and other relationships among inflation, unemployment, and profit rates can be calculated directly from the appropriate partial derivatives of Equation 3.15:

$$\partial c_t/\partial R_t = 0.67$$
$$\partial c_t/\partial p_t = -1.58$$
$$\partial c_t/\partial U_t = -23.24\, U_t^{-2}$$
$$\partial U_t/\partial R_t = 0.029\, U_t^{2}$$

(3.16)

## Some Qualifications

In the final chapter of this book, some of the formal results just developed will be reconsidered and discussed in the light of their relevance to policy. It is useful to suggest some of the needed qualifications now.

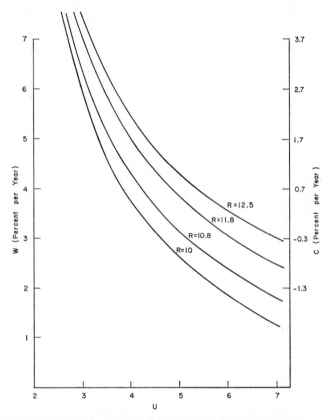

FIGURE 3.8c.   *Final wage change-unemployment-inflation relation* (from Equation 3.8, for each of four profit rates *R*), with productivity growing at 3.3 percent annually.

The implications for price behavior have been drawn partly from an estimated wage relation and partly from a neutral standard relating prices and wages via productivity. Actual price behavior may not conform to this standard. In particular, the widely held assumption that prices are relatively inflexible downward, if true, would bias price movements upward from the neutral standard, particularly when the standard called for stable or falling average prices. Since the standard implies that prices in industries with above average productivity growth will fall relative to the average, the failure of these prices to fall will raise the average change above the predicted level, both directly and via its impact back on wages through living costs and possibly profit rates.

Similarly, the existence of industries whose wage and price be-

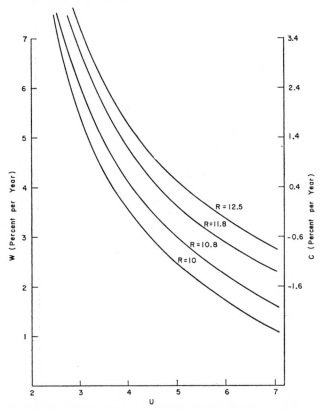

FIGURE 3.8d. *Final wage change-unemployment-inflation relation* (from Equation 3.8, for each of four profit rates R), with productivity growing at 3.6 per cent annually.

havior does not conform to the estimates made here for manufacturing will alter the relations just described, again both directly and indirectly. Again, the common presumption is that where there are such industries, they display price behavior that is biased upward.

It is important to note, however, that while these qualifications may alter the present estimate of such things as the *level* of unemployment required for average price stability, they *improve* the *trade-off* between less unemployment and more rapid price increase. Once the price behavior of some sectors is fixed exogenously, as it is to some degree in the two cases just cited, it becomes costless, as far as these sectors is concerned, to push unemployment lower. Hence it costs less, in terms of average price increase, to do so than

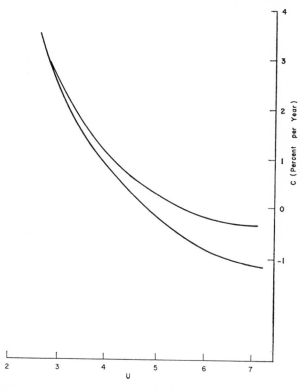

FIGURE 3.9. *Adjustment to inflation relation required if some prices are rigid downward.*

Solid line — Change in typical relation due to downward price rigidities in some sectors.

Broken line — Typical relation from wage equation as in Figures 3.8*a, b, c, d.*

the previous analysis would suggest. The aggregate price–profit-rate–unemployment schedule is not only raised so that *average* relations are worsened (more inflationary) at least over some range, but it is also tilted by the same arguments, so that the *marginal* relations improve.

Consider first the case in which prices in some industries are assumed to be rigid downward. For rates of wage increase slower than productivity gains in such industries, the calculations just made would call for price declines, and the actual situation would therefore show more rapid average price increases than do those calculations. On the other hand, moving to successively more rapid rates of wage increase would involve smaller increments to the rate of price increase than the calculations show, since those prices still determined by the downward rigidity constraint would behave no differently than they would have with less rapid wage increases. The calculated prediction of wage behavior would prevail only after wage changes exceeded productivity gains everywhere, so that the constraint of downward rigidity was nowhere present. And it is only beyond this point that the trade-off between unemployment and average price increases would be as steep as calculated. Figure 3.9 illustrates the type of adjustment to the Figure 3.8 diagrams that these conditions would require. Whether there is much empirical relevance to downward price rigidities is another question that is in no way explored or implied here.

Now consider the case in which prices in some industries are assumed at no time to behave in the way described by the present equations for manufacturing. To take an extreme case, assume half of all prices rise autonomously by 2.0 percent a year, while prices elsewhere are governed by the wage relation together with the productivity arithmetic that has been used to link wage and price behavior. In this case, the aggregate price index would change by the average of the changes in the two groups, or by

$$c_t = \tfrac{1}{2} \left[ (w_t - p_t) + 2.0 \right]. \tag{3.17}$$

Using the wage relation for $w_t$, the aggregate price equation equivalent to Equation 3.15 where all prices followed the wage-relation–productivity calculations is now

$$c_t = -1.4 - 0.62\, p_t + 9.0\, U_t^{-1} + 0.26\, R_t. \tag{3.18}$$

Figure 3.10 illustrates the type of adjustment to a typical curve from the Figure 3.8 diagrams that these new conditions require. Where Figure 3.8 calls for less than a 2.0 percent rate of price rise, the aggregate price index would now rise more than calculated;

while when the earlier calculations call for more than a 2.0 percent
increase, actual price increase would now average less than this.
The slope of the relation between rates of price increase and unemployment would be less than half of that indicated by the Figure
3.8 calculations; the trade-off between inflation and unemployment
would be considerably less severe than those calculations suggest.
Of course, the actual adjustment illustrated by Figure 3.10 and
Equation 3.18 is only illustrative and has no empirical foundation.

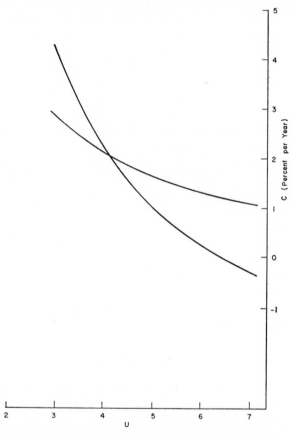

FIGURE 3.10. *Adjustment to inflation relation required if some prices
are determined autonomously.*
Solid line — Predicted by wage relation alone from Figure 3.8*b*, with R =
11.8.
Broken line — Predicted if half of all prices rise autonomously while the
other half follow from the wage relation.

### The Cost-of-Living Term

The cost-of-living coefficient in Equation 3.8 is 0.367. This is well below one and lower than the previous estimate of 0.466 in Equation 3.5, where unemployment was the only additional explanatory variable. Since both the wage and cost-of-living variables are expressed as annual percentage changes,[18] the coefficient gives the elasticity between the two variables. Thus a given change in the cost of living will lead, one quarter later, to a little over one third this percentage change in the wage rate. This is in contrast to the sometimes expressed view that this elasticity should be one. Such a view is implicit, for instance, in any theory that asserts the real wage is the appropriate dependent variable for analysis.

In discussing Equation 3.5, the cost-of-living coefficient there was compared with the equivalent estimates from some of the studies for Britain. It now appears that the estimate of Equation 3.5 was too high because of the omission of the other explanatory variables that appear in Equation 3.8. It seems likely that the estimates of the other studies may also be too high for the same reason.

[18] The cost-of-living variable is actually the sum of four one-quarter changes. But disregarding the small differences in the denominator term for each quarter, the cost-of-living variable is equal to the annual percentage change in the cost of living.

# 4

# The Wage Relation over Time
# and the Predictive Ability
# of the Postwar Relation

## Introduction

This chapter examines the behavior of the wage relation over time and tests some conjectures that arise from this examination. First an intraperiod analysis is conducted for the postwar years. This includes a test of the stability of the relation over the period and a tentative exploration of the impact of long-term unemployment on wages. Then a comparison of the postwar period and the 1920's is made. Finally, the postwar relation is tested as a predictor of wage changes in the years since the sample period from which the equation was estimated.

## An Intraperiod Analysis of the Postwar Years

The residuals from Equation 3.8 are plotted in Figure 4.1. These show no evidence of correlation with the business cycle, indicating the explanatory variables successfully account for the marked variations in rates of wage change over the cycle. The residuals do exhibit serial correlation, as expected from the four-quarter span of the dependent variable. And somewhat less expectedly, they show a preponderance of underestimates in the latter half of the postwar period.

The year 1953 marked a transition point for the postwar economy in several respects. It marked the end of hostilities in Korea. It was the year when price and wage scrutiny by the government ceased. It was the last year for several temporary taxes on incomes, including the excess profits tax. It was the first of eight years of Republican administration in Washington. And it was the last year the unemployment rate came anywhere near 3.0 percent. Together with the evidence of the residuals, these facts suggest the postwar period should be divided at about this time in order to investigate possible shifts in the relation under study. The cutoff point was chosen after the second quarter of 1953. This is before the residuals turned predominantly positive, but coincides with the other objective factors just cited.

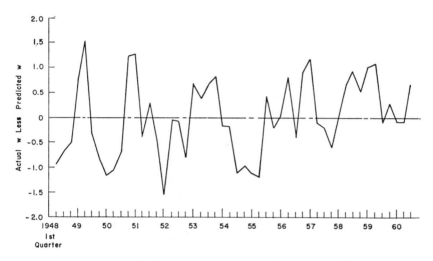

FIGURE 4.1.    *Residuals from wage equation (Equation 3.8).*

Table 4.1 gives the mean values of all explanatory values and $w_t$ for the first 21 quarters, up to the second quarter of 1953, and for the remaining 29 quarters covered by the study. All the variables except $\Delta R_t$ have larger mean values in the earlier period. The difference in the mean of $w_t$ between the two periods is 1.853. Using the coefficient estimates for the whole period, we can see how much of this difference is accounted for by changes in the explanatory variables and how much is left to be accounted for by differences in the actual coefficient and constant-term estimates.

Using the coefficient estimates of Equation 3.8, the difference in the mean of $R_{t-1}$ shown in Table 4.1 accounts for 1.034 of the difference in the mean of $w_t$; the difference in the mean of $c_{t-1}$ accounts for 0.734 more; that in the mean of $U_t{}^{-1}$ for another 0.549; and the difference in the mean of $\Delta R_t$ makes a negative contribution, accounting for —0.141. The sum of these individual components comes to 2.175, which is more than the observed change in the mean of $w_t$. The balance is accounted for by the excess of over-

TABLE 4.1
MEAN VALUES OF ALL VARIABLES BEFORE AND AFTER MID-1953

| Variable | Mean Values of Variables | |
|---|---|---|
| | Up to 1953 2Q | After 1953 2Q |
| $U_t{}^{-1}$ | 0.251 | 0.214 |
| $c_{t-1}$ | 3.419 | 1.419 |
| $R_{t-1}$ | 13.217 | 10.781 |
| $\Delta R_t$ | — 0.224 | — 0.047 |
| $w_t$ | 5.879 | 4.026 |

estimates from Equation 3.8 in this period, as measured by the negative residuals.

*Regressions for Each Subperiod*

In order to get some insight into the possible reasons for these observations, separate regressions were estimated for the first and second half of the postwar period, using mid-1953 as the dividing point. Because these two subperiods are so short, the reliability of the resulting estimates, including the standard errors, is questionable. About all that can be claimed is that they offer evidence on the likely direction of change in parameters between the two periods. For most purposes, such as predicting outside the sample period, the average relation for all the postwar years may be safer, although this judgment must depend in part on what one believes are the causes of any observed difference between the subperiods. Still, if the subperiods are to be examined, the equations for each are the best tools available. The estimates for the two subperiods were quite different:

for 1948–1953,

$$w_t = -17.626 - \underset{(0.092)}{0.025}\, c_{t-1} + \underset{(4.731)}{33.954}\, U_t{}^{-1} + \underset{(0.156)}{1.156}\, R_{t-1}$$
$$+ \underset{(0.172)}{1.000}\, \Delta R_t + e_t, \qquad R^2 = 0.953; \qquad (4.1)$$

and for 1953–1960,

$$w_t = -4.712 + \underset{(0.132)}{0.680} \, c_{t-1} + \underset{(3.050)}{18.421} \, U_t^{-1} + \underset{(0.120)}{0.360} \, R_{t-1}$$

$$+ \underset{(0.300)}{1.244} \, \Delta R_t + e_t, \qquad R^2 = 0.800. \qquad (4.2)$$

The most striking difference is in the coefficient for the cost-of-living term, $c_{t-1}$. In the first period, this is negative but in fact insignificantly different from zero. It seems safe to assume the true coefficient is positive. Even so, the estimates indicate it is almost certainly smaller than the same coefficient for the second period. The $U_t^{-1}$ and $R_{t-1}$ coefficients, on the other hand, are both larger in the first period than in the second.

The relative explanatory importance of the different variables in the two periods can be assessed directly by comparing their squared partial correlation coefficients. This is done in Table 4.2. The big

TABLE 4.2

SQUARED PARTIAL CORRELATION COEFFICIENTS[*]

IN TWO SUBPERIODS

| Variable | First Period | Second Period |
|----------|-------------|---------------|
| $c_{t-1}$ | 0.005 | 0.526 |
| $R_{t-1}$ | 0.773 | 0.274 |
| $\Delta R_t$ | 0.682 | 0.417 |
| $U_t^{-1}$ | 0.764 | 0.603 |

[*] Not corrected for degrees of freedom.

changes shown in the table are in the $c_{t-1}$ and $R_{t-1}$ variables, whose squared partial correlation coefficients go from 0.005 to 0.526 and from 0.773 to 0.274 respectively. In the first period, the simple correlations between these variables is 0.638; and in the second period, it is only —0.047. This high simple correlation in the first period helps account for the weak independent effect estimated for $c_{t-1}$ and for the small negative coefficient estimated for it.[1] The independent explanatory power of the other two variables, $\Delta R_t$ and $U_t^{-1}$, stays relatively unchanged in the two periods, although in both cases it is higher in the first. Although the quantitative esti-

[1] The simple correlation of $c_{t-1}$ with $U_t^{-1}$ in the first period is 0.488, also fairly high. The correlation of $c_{t-1}$ with $w_t$ is a surprising 0.862—surprising in view of their negligible partial correlation in the regression.

mates may be of doubtful reliability, these results do suggest the probable directions of change. And there is some fairly direct interpretation for most of these results.

The much stronger effect of the cost of living on wages in the second period can be associated with the increased importance of cost-of-living clauses in wage contracts. The actual history of cost-of-living clauses has been somewhat erratic, although it does support the generalization that such clauses have been more important after 1953 than before. This is because in the earlier period they came into prominence only after the start of the Korean War; they were a significant factor throughout the latter period.

Before the outbreak of the Korean War, cost-of-living provisions in manufacturing were present only in the General Motors agreement with the United Auto Workers Union and a scattering of numerically unimportant lesser contracts. The war and the fear of inflation associated with it made them popular, and by its end approximately 3.5 million workers, or one fifth of those whose wages were set by collective agreements, had cost-of-living provisions in their contracts.[2] This total includes all workers and not only those in manufacturing industries. By 1955, the number of workers covered by such provisions was down to about 1.7 million, but 1 million of the reduction from the Korean War peak came from railroad workers.[3] By the end of 1956, coverage was back to 3.5 million as the railroad workers and others came back to cost-of-living provisions,[4] and in 1959 the number rose to 4 million.[5]

From these considerations, one might expect to find the importance of the cost-of-living term increase between the two subperiods. But one might also expect its true value to be significantly positive in the early period, contrary to the estimate in Equation 4.1.[6]

The exceptional importance of $R_{t-1}$ in the early period may be attributed to the two unusual circumstances that dominated that

---

[2] *Monthly Labor Review*, March 1955, p. 314.

[3] *Ibid.*, p. 316.

[4] *Monthly Labor Review*, January 1957, p. 52.

[5] *Monthly Labor Review*, December 1960, p. 1270.

[6] For example, even if the estimated standard error were correct, the coefficient estimate were unbiased, and the true value of the coefficient of $c_{t-1}$ in the first period were $+0.05$, one would still expect to find an estimate of this coefficient as small as $-0.025$ almost 25 percent of the time. A much larger value is not unlikely considering what has already been said about the reliability of the subperiod estimates being discussed.

period. In the first years, the economy was still adjusting to postwar conditions. Controls during the war had allowed considerable disequilibrium to develop in the wage-profit relationship, and profit rates were exceptionally high. Under these conditions, wages changes may have been particularly sensitive to the level of profit rates as labor attempted to correct this disequilibrium. In the latter years of the period, the Korean War dominated the economy, and once again the link of wage changes with profit rates, or at least their apparent link, may have become tighter than otherwise as wages and prices, and hence profits, all rose rapidly in anticipation of possible controls. Such arguments about the connection between wage changes and profits in the first period lend themselves to the use of a threshhold effect in profits or a nonlinear relation between the variables. However, neither possibility was investigated here.

### The Inflationary Structure of the Two Subperiods

The two periods were further compared by putting the mean values of the variables for each period into the estimated equations for the other period. This allowed a comparison of the actual wage changes that occurred in each case with the changes that would have occurred if the estimated equations from the other period had prevailed. Using the data from the second period in the equation for the first gave a predicted average annual wage change of 2.03 percent per year, compared with the actual average change in the second period of 4.03. Using the first-period data in the second-period equation gave a predicted average annual wage change of 6.73 percent, compared with the actual value of 5.89 for the first period. By both measures, the relation estimated for the second period appears more inflationary. However, owing to the presence of several explanatory variables in each equation, such a finding requires qualification.

The main reason the second subperiod appears more inflationary than the first is the sharply higher estimate for the impact of living costs on wages. This has the effect of increasing the slope in the kind of wage change-unemployment relation plotted in Figure 3.8. Again using the relation that rates of price change will, on the average, equal the difference between rates of wage change and productivity increase, we can solve the price-change terms out of Equations 4.1 and 4.2. For the steady state case, this yields the following results:

for 1948–1953 (with the living-cost coefficient taken as zero),

$$w_t = -17.6 + 34.0\, U_t{}^{-1} + 1.2\, R_t; \qquad (4.3)$$

and for 1953–1960,

$$w_t = -14.5 - 2.1\, \rho_t + 57.1\, U_t{}^{-1} + 1.1\, R_t. \qquad (4.4)$$

Since the cost-of-living term feeds back into the wage-change estimate in this kind of equation, its effect is highlighted. With a profit rate of 10.8 percent, the average for the 1953–1960 period, and productivity increases of 3 percent annually, Equation 4.3 predicts annual wage increases of 6.7 percent with 3 percent unemployment, 3.9 percent with 4 percent unemployment, and 1.7 percent with 6 percent unemployment. The corresponding estimates using Equation 4.4 are 10.1 percent, 5.4 percent, and 0.6 percent. So the relation for the second subperiod is more steeply sloped relative to the first rather than unambiguously more inflationary. However, it would predict more rapid wage increases for those values of the explanatory variables that would be expected in periods of low unemployment.

Perhaps what is more important, these calculations further highlight the likely inaccuracy of the estimates for the individual subperiods. The complete absence of an effect from living costs in the first equation has already been questioned. Now the size of the estimate for that coefficient in the second subperiod's equation appears entirely too large when one considers its effect on the slope of the wage change-unemployment trade-off as exemplified in Equation 4.4 and the calculations made previously.[7]

### Significance Tests on the Subperiods

Questioning the accuracy of the relations estimated for each subperiod is not equivalent to denying that the relations do differ. The estimates available for each period are different, and there remains the question of whether the apparent differences are significant. It is hard to say what importance should be attached to standard statistical tests conducted on relations that are thought *a priori* to be inaccurate. In comparing Equations 4.1 and 4.2, the *a priori* judgment that follows from the previous discussion is that the coefficient estimates differ by more than they would if both

---

[7] Where Equation 4.4 yields 10.1 percent and 0.6 percent for the predicted wage changes at 3 percent and 6 percent unemployment, the equivalent calculations based on Equation 3.8 predicted 6.4 percent and 2.5 percent as one can read off of Figure 3.8b.

equations were best unbiased estimates. Therefore the results of a statistical test that assumes unbiased estimates should be acceptable if they suggest observed differences are *not* significant; but the results carry unknown authority if they conclude the differences *are* significant at some level of probability.

No tests on the individual coefficients were attempted, but the regressions as a whole were compared for the two subperiods. The test used was one described by Gregory C. Chow.[8] For this test, the null hypothesis is that two linear regressions are both estimates of the same structural relations. Chow shows that if the null hypothesis is true, the ratio of the difference between the sum of squares of residuals when a single regression covers all the data and the sum of squares of residuals from the two separate regressions, over the sum of squares of residuals from the two separate regressions, with both numerator and denominator adjusted for their numbers of degrees of freedom, will have an $F$ distribution.

The null hypothesis in our case is that the 1948–1953 and 1953–1960 periods are both described by the same structural relation for wage determination. Using the number of quarterly observations to measure the numbers of degrees of freedom, this hypothesis is rejected at the 0.99 percent level of significance for a value of the ratio greater than 3.51. The ratio actually calculated was 6.03, so the hypothesis is rejected. In view of the preceding remarks, this offers further evidence of a difference in the relation governing the two periods; but our certainty about such a difference is less than the test would suggest.

### Residuals: The Habitually Unemployed

Besides the possible difference between the first and second part of the postwar period that they suggest, the residuals from Equation 3.8 also reveal a possible difference in the reaction of wages to long-term unemployment as compared with purely cyclical unemployment. Starting with the 1958 recession, the residuals are positive for the rest of the quarters in the study, except for three when they are very slightly negative, indicating the period is characterized by underestimates of wage changes. Using Equation 4.2, estimated for the 1953–1960 period alone, the pattern holds even more strikingly, with only one negative residual observed after the onset of the 1958

[8] Chow, Gregory C., "Tests of Equality Between Sets of Coefficients in Two Linear Regressions," *Econometrica*, Vol. 28 (July 1960).

recession. The hypothesis suggested by these facts is that the unemployment measured for the years starting with 1958 is higher than that which is appropriate for explaining wage behavior.

The recovery from the 1958 recession was abortive. The unemployment rate in no quarter after 1957 fell below 5 percent, and long-term unemployment rates remained above the levels of previous recoveries. A pool of habitually unemployed apparently developed as a result of the failure of aggregate demand to rise far enough. It may be that this group became so removed from the active labor market that it had no impact on wage changes. In this case, the appropriate measure of unemployment for the purpose of this study would exclude this group. To test this hypothesis, 1 percentage point was dropped from all unemployment figures starting in 1958, and the resulting series was used to measure unemployment in the active part of the labor force that influences wage behavior. A regression using this new unemployment concept was run for the postwar period with the following results, where $U_t^*$ is now the new unemployment series:

$$w_t = -5.08 + \underset{(0.053)}{0.365\, c_{t-1}} + \underset{(2.134)}{14.821\, U_t^{-1}} + \underset{(0.068)}{0.464\, R_{t-1}}$$

$$+ \underset{(0.172)}{0.880\, \Delta R_t} + e_t, \qquad R^2 = 0.874. \qquad (4.5)$$

The percentage of variation explained by the regression goes up slightly compared with Equation 3.8, from 0.870 to 0.874. The individual coefficients also change only slightly, with all but the one for $c_{t-1}$ showing increases. A more interesting observation is that *all* the partial correlation coefficients are improved, even if only a little: that for the $c_{t-1}$ term goes from 0.508 to 0.513; that for the $U_t^{-1}$ term from 0.501 to 0.516; that for the $R_{t-1}$ term from 0.456 to 0.508; and that for the $\Delta R_t$ term from 0.316 to 0.364. Since the change in the unemployment series was prompted by the appearance of the residuals from the original equation, it was almost certain to yield some over-all improvement. But the evidence that the change sharpens the explanatory role of all the variables suggests that it is a real, if small, improvement in the specification of the unemployment variable relevant for explaining wage behavior.

The residuals from Equation 4.5 reflect the adjustment that was made, although the previous pattern is only partly removed. The 1958 recession still shows underestimates in its first five quarters as it did before; but following that, the residuals are mixed.

More careful attempts to take account of the possibly special character of the habitually unemployed might yield considerably more information about their impact on the economy and particularly on wage determination. Alternatives to the method tried here that would still deal with the problem at an aggregated level might be to use data explicitly on long-term unemployment or on total unemployment in distressed areas. The present hypothesis has simply been that part of the unemployed may become so insulated from the active part of the labor force that they have little or no impact on wage changes. This hypothesis allows for many possible reasons why they become so insulated, and the appropriate way to take account of this group may depend on the reasons that are in fact true.

It is important to stress that this hypothesis about the special character of the habitually unemployed refers only to the impact of this group on aggregate wage levels. It does not imply that this group is different in any other respects. In particular, it does not suggest that normal remedies for unemployment would be ineffective. Depending on other characteristics, such as the extent to which the habitually unemployed are concentrated in isolated distressed areas, general remedies will be more or less effective in reaching the unemployed. The hypothesis does suggest that if this group can be reached by selective remedies, it represents a promising source of increased real output with little or no social cost in the form of increased inflationary pressure on wages.

### An Historical Comparison

One major point that deserves attention in a study of wage determination is how the recent past compares with earlier periods. Particularly in view of the great changes that have taken place in the wage-setting institutions of the economy, it is of interest to know whether the reaction of wages to other economic variables has changed. In Chapter 1, it was noted that A. W. Phillips found his relation between wage changes and unemployment in Great Britain remarkably stable over time, although the work of subsequent authors cast some doubt on this result. This section will deal with a similar question for the United States. But since the model presented here rejects a theory of wage determination based on unemployment alone, our interest will be in the relation of wage changes to all the explanatory variables found important in the study of the post-World War II period.

The period of the 1920's was picked for comparison with the post-World War II years. Most of the 1930's and the war years that followed were dominated too much by special circumstances surrounding wage rates to yield a ready comparison with other periods. The 1930's saw the enactment of important new legislation in the labor relations field, while during the war, wages and prices were under control by the federal government. Prior to the 1920's, data were not available for a suitable estimate of the wage-determination relation used here.

The availability of data for the 1920's also raised problems, but they were not insurmountable. Suitable series were available for profit rate, unemployment, wages, and living costs, but only on an annual basis for the first three of these. Therefore it was necessary to approximate the timing relations specified in the model by combining the annual observations in a particular way. The result involved some loss of information and precision, but still allowed a rough test of the 1920's period.

### Data for the 1920's

The unemployment series used was that compiled by Stanley Lebergott.[9] His series gave annual unemployment in the civilian labor force.[10] In establishing a timing relation, it was assumed that the series most nearly approximated the average unemployment of the four quarters of each year.

The series for profit rate after taxes in manufacturing industries was taken from Ralph C. Epstein.[11] It is based on 2,046 manufacturing corporations which received from 57 to 63 percent of the total income of firms in this category. The profit rates are given annually, and again the figures are assumed to represent the average of four quarters in each year.

For the cost of living, the Consumer Price Index, published by the Department of Labor, was available on a monthly basis for the 1920's. This series was aggregated to a quarterly basis and then used to compute percentage changes just as for the 1947–1960 period.

The wage-rate series used was constructed by Albert Rees and

[9] Lebergott, Stanley, "Annual Estimates of Unemployment in the United States, 1900–1954," *The Measurement and Behavior of Unemployment* (Princeton, N.J.: Princeton University Press, 1957), pp. 215–216.

[10] The data presented there were multiplied by 1.1 to make them comparable with the current definitions used in the 1947–1960 data of this paper.

[11] Epstein, Ralph C., *Industrial Profits in the United States* (National Bureau of Economic Research, Inc., New York, 1934), p. 56.

published in *Wages, Prices, Profits and Productivity*.[12] This series gives average earnings per hour at work for production workers in manufacturing industries. It specifically includes the effect on the actual pay rate of fringe benefits and pay received for time not worked, such as sick leave and holidays; but changes in these factors were not important in the 1920's period. The Rees series gives annual data, which were assumed to represent the figures in the middle of each year. The percentage changes in these figures were calculated and treated as representing percentage changes of successive midyear points.

In order to approximate the desired timing relationships between the variables, the average of each two successive years' figures was taken to represent the desired variables in both the profit-rate and unemployment series. By the interpretation of the original series just described, these new variables were taken to represent the profit-rate and unemployment rate of four-quarter periods ending in the middle of each year. The change in profit rate was calculated as the first difference of this new profit-rate series. The cost-of-living index was used with the percentage changes measured from successive second-quarter points so that the relationship of that variable to profit rate was the same as in the 1947–1960 analysis. Since the percentage changes in the wage-rate series were taken to be dated at successive midyear points, the resultant timing relationship between it and the explanatory variables was approximately correct. The variables that should have led wage changes by one quarter were instead contemporaneous with it; but considering the rough assumptions used to estimate timing, this difference is probably insignificant.

### The Two Periods Compared

The time series of the variables used for the 1920's as just described are given in Table 4.3. The available data permitted only construction of series for the years 1920 through 1928. The explanatory variables from this table were used in Equation 3.8 to get the values of $w_t$ predicted by that equation. Table 4.4 gives these predicted values together with the actual values of $w_t$ for each year and the difference between the two.

The first thing to notice about the results in Table 4.4 is the pre-

[12] Rees, Albert, "Patterns of Wages, Prices and Productivity" in *Wages, Prices, Profits and Productivity* (The American Assembly, Columbia University, 1959), p. 15.

dominance of overpredictions that results from using Equation 3.8, estimated for 1948–1960, to predict wage change in the 1920's. The mean difference of the actual and predicted values is —1.43. It appears that for given values of the explanatory variables, wage changes were considerably greater in the recent period than in the 1920's. This may be viewed as an inflationary bias in the recent

TABLE 4.3

ACTUAL PERCENTAGE WAGE CHANGE AND ITS EXPLANATORY
VARIABLES FOR THE 1920's

| Year | $c_t$ | $R_t$ | $U_t{-1}$ | $\Delta R_t$ | $w_t$ |
|------|-------|-------|-----------|--------------|-------|
| 1920 | + 22.6 | 11.4 | 0.290 | — 1.8 | + 12.60 |
| 1921 | — 13.6 | 5.8 | 0.114 | — 5.6 | — 13.60 |
| 1922 | —  6.2 | 5.5 | 0.093 | — 0.3 | —  6.25 |
| 1923 | +  1.5 | 9.6 | 0.168 | + 4.1 | + 10.10 |
| 1924 | +  0.3 | 9.5 | 0.211 | — 0.1 | +  3.97 |
| 1925 | +  1.9 | 9.8 | 0.192 | + 0.3 | —  0.20 |
| 1926 | +  2.7 | 10.9 | 0.308 | + 1.1 | +  1.21 |
| 1927 | —  2.1 | 9.6 | 0.303 | — 1.3 | +  1.39 |
| 1928 | —  1.6 | 9.0 | 0.215 | — 0.6 | +  0.59 |

TABLE 4.4

PREDICTED* AND ACTUAL WAGE CHANGES, 1920–1928

| Year | Actual | Predicted* | Difference |
|------|--------|-----------|------------|
| 1920 | + 12.60 | + 11.65 | + 0.95 |
| 1921 | — 13.60 | —  9.63 | — 3.97 |
| 1922 | —  6.25 | —  1.63 | — 4.63 |
| 1923 | + 10.10 | +  5.96 | + 4.95 |
| 1924 | +  3.97 | +  2.82 | + 1.15 |
| 1925 | —  0.20 | +  3.64 | — 3.84 |
| 1926 | +  1.21 | +  6.63 | — 5.42 |
| 1927 | +  1.39 | +  2.42 | — 1.03 |
| 1928 | +  0.59 | +  1.58 | — 0.99 |

* Predicted using Equation 3.8 with explanatory variables in Table 4.3.

period relative to the former one, possibly attributable to the increased strength of labor's bargaining power. But in fact such a judgment ought to be reserved until the wage-change figures are considered together with data on the trend rate of productivity increase.

Albert Rees has compiled estimates of output per production worker man-hour in manufacturing[13] that permit productivity com-

[13] Rees, *ibid.*, p. 15.

parisons between the two periods.[14] From 1920 to 1928, this series shows an average annual rate of increase of 5.5 percent, while from 1948 to 1957, the latest date Rees uses, the rate is 3.4 percent. Therefore, these productivity figures confirm the previous judgment that the wage-determination relation has become more inflationary in the post-World War II period as compared with the 1920's.

One possible objection to the foregoing analysis might be that the early part of the 1920's was a highly atypical period, dominated first by a sharp postwar inflation and then by a severe recession, and that judgments about the whole period should exclude these years since they may disproportionately influence the results. However, although it may thus be appropriate to drop these years for some purposes, the conclusions reached thus far are not affected by doing so. The predominance of overestimates shown in Table 4.4 is still evident if only the remainder of the period is considered.

Two tests were conducted next to determine whether the apparent differences between the 1920's and post-World War II years provided statistically significant evidence of a change in the structural relation between the two periods. The first test used was the one described earlier in the discussion of the intraperiod comparison for the postwar period.

First a regression was run applying the wage model to the data of the 1920's. The result was the following estimated equation:

$$w_t = 5.69 + \underset{(0.23)}{0.48\, c_t} - \underset{(39.15)}{3.64\, U^{-1}} + \underset{(2.12)}{0.88\, R_t} + \underset{(0.68)}{1.12\, \Delta R_t}\, e_t,$$

$$R^2 = 0.90. \qquad (4.6)$$

With only nine observations, these estimates have little value in themselves, but they were needed for the first test used. Another regression was performed using just second-quarter observations from the postwar years so that both periods were described by comparable annual observations. The result of this regression for the postwar years was

$$w_t = -4.206 + \underset{(0.111)}{0.259\, c_{t-1}} + \underset{(4.718)}{14.588\, U_t{}^{-1}} + \underset{(0.148)}{0.436\, R_{t-1}}$$

$$+ \underset{(0.340)}{0.240\, \Delta R} + e_t, \qquad R^2 = 0.887. \qquad (4.7)$$

Finally, a regression was performed using the annual data for the

---

[14] We are interested here in the relative performance of the two periods and use Rees' series because it is convenient for this comparison.

1920's together with the second-quarter observations from the post-war period. The estimated equation in this case was

$$w_t = -5.688 + 0.451\,c_{t-1} + 9.408\,U_t{}^{-1} + 0.584\,R_{t-1}$$
$$\quad\quad\quad (0.092)\quad\quad\ (8.439)\quad\quad\quad (0.228)$$
$$+ 1.136\,\Delta R_t + e_t, \quad R^2 = 0.885. \quad\quad (4.8)$$
$$(0.272)$$

The three regression equations, 4.6, 4.7, and 4.8, were used in the test.

The hypothesis tested was again that the two periods in question were characterized by the same structural relations explaining wage determination. For the present regressions, this hypothesis is rejected at the 95 percent probability level for values of the test statistic greater than 3.11. The value of the test statistic actually calculated from the sum of squared residuals of Equations 4.6, 4.7, and 4.8 was only 0.561; therefore the test failed to reject the hypothesis at the 95 percent probability level.

Failure to reject does not constitute positive evidence for accepting the hypothesis. And since it seemed possible that the failure to reject may have been due to the extreme observations of the early 1920's, a second test was tried. This compared only the later years with the postwar period, so that the comparison would not be dominated by the presence of the extreme observations from 1920 through 1923. This test is described by Chow[15] and differs from the previous one in that no regression is calculated for the short period —in the present case 1924 through 1928—since there are not enough observations to do so. Again, the null hypothesis is that the two periods were characterized by the same structural relation explaining wage changes. This hypothesis is rejected at the 0.99 probability level for values of the test statistic greater than 6.63. In this case the statistic was 8.15, so that the null hypothesis is firmly rejected. The test shows that the 1924–1928 period was characterized by a different structure than the post-World War II years and fortifies the earlier observations and discussion of the differences between the two periods.

### Predicting Wage Change

Since the original regressions were run, three years of data have become available for testing the predictive ability of the wage re-

[15] Chow, *op. cit.*

lation. Figure 4.2 plots actual percentage wage changes alongside those estimated from Equation 3.8 over the period for which the regression was run and for the thirteen quarters following the original sample period. Although errors are grouped in these thirteen quarters of prediction, being first consistently negative and then consistently positive, the predictions over the whole period seem satisfactory. Some serial correlation of the errors is to be expected, and the negative and positive errors do roughly balance

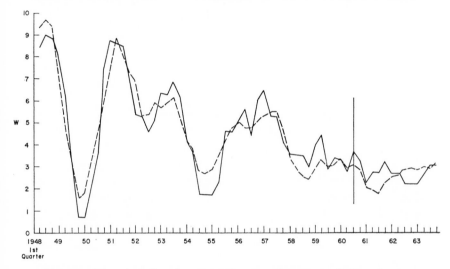

FIGURE 4.2.   *Actual and estimated wage changes, including the forecast period.*
Solid line — Actual.
Broken line — Predicted from Equation 3.8.

by the end of the prediction period. The standard error of estimation for the thirteen predicted quarters is 0.57 compared with a standard error of estimation of 0.77 in the original regression.

When the model is translated into a prediction of wage-rate *levels*, the forecasts appear quite satisfactory. In no quarter is the error greater than 2 cents per hour, and at the end of the thirteenth quarter of prediction there is no error. Predictions of the wage-rate level are compared with actual values in Figure 4.3.

When Equation 4.5 is used, with its adjustment for the habitually unemployed, the prediction pattern is similar to that in Figure 4.2. Beginning in 1962, faster wage increases are predicted than with Equation 3.8, but the pattern of movement is otherwise the same.

Thus the overestimates that characterize the last half of the thirteen prediction quarters are more pronounced than with Equation 3.8, and predicted values of wage change still exceed actual values at the end of the period (by about 0.3 percentage points of annual wage change).

It is possible to offer some *ex post* speculation about the errors in the prediction period. Recorded labor force growth during 1962

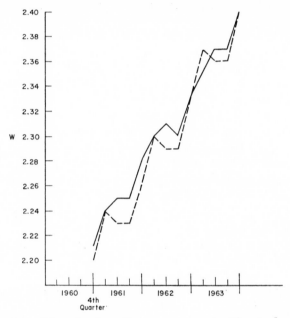

FIGURE 4.3.   *Wage-level predictions compared with actual wage levels in the forecast period, using Equation 3.8 (for quarters beyond the fitted period).*
Solid line — Actual.
Broken line — Estimate.

fell substantially behind the growth projected from demographic factors. Since the labor force is the denominator of the unemployment-rate statistic, to the extent this participation-rate shortfall was extraordinary, a normal unemployment reading for the period would have been larger and would have predicted slower wage changes. To gauge the possible magnitude of such an effect, the recorded employment for 1962 together with a civilian labor force 400,000 greater than recorded would have made the 1962 unemployment rate 6.1 percent rather than the 5.6 percent actually recorded. In

Equation 3.8, a change of this size would lower the estimated percentage increase in wage rates by 0.24 percentage points.

An adjustment in the other direction may be appropriate to take account of the revision in depreciation guidelines that became effective in mid-1962. By the time these were fully applicable, they amounted to a decrease in stated profits, and hence profit rates, of roughly 5 percent. From Equation 3.8, such an understatement would lead to an underprediction of wage changes of roughly 0.2 percentage points if it is assumed that what should count is the profit-rate figure based on the old depreciation rules. And this takes account only of the term for the level of profit rates, ignoring the transitory effect of the $\Delta R$ term in Equation 3.8.

The other factor to consider in connection with the present results is the increased activity of the Kennedy-Johnson Administrations in the wage-price field, starting with the introduction of wage-price guidelines in 1962.[16] With or without the adjustment of the previous paragraphs, the tendency for underestimates by the wage equations has not been present since the middle of 1962. This may be the first sign of some success for the Administration's attempt to moderate the inflationary tendencies of the economy.

[16] *Economic Report of the President, January 1962* (Washington, D. C.: U.S. Government Printing Office, 1962).

# 5

# A Wage-Price-Profit Subsystem
# and Its Dynamic Properties

### Introduction

In Chapter 2, the study of aggregate wage behavior started with
the formulation of a model describing the effect of certain explanatory variables on the rate of change of money wage rates. Chapters
3 and 4 used the wage-change equation specified by this model to
estimate the coefficients of the explanatory variables for various
periods, and to test the explanatory power of the model and of the
individual variables. Variations on the basic equation were also
tested, and some of the implications of the estimates were discussed.
The analysis of those chapters was confined to these variations on
the wage-change equation, and the statistical estimation method
used was simple least squares.

The present chapter considers the basic wage-change equation
as one part of a more general wage-price-profit subsystem for the
economy. Equations are estimated explaining profit rates, manufacturing output prices, and living costs. Together with the wage
equation, these permit some dynamic analysis of the inflation question which takes more explicit account than was possible until now
of the lagged effect of wages on prices and profits and the feedback
of these to wages again. It is possible to establish the dynamic
stability of this system which helps validate the preceding analysis
of comparative steady states in Chapters 3 and 4.

The introduction of relations explaining prices and profits also
offers an opportunity to use an alternative estimating technique to
compare with simple least-squares estimates. For reasons to be
discussed, the preferred forms of the wage-price-profit equations
are not treated in this way. But a variation of these, consisting of

dropping all the lags from the preferred equations, is estimated using two-stage least squares, a consistent estimating technique. These estimates turn out to be almost identical to the simple least-squares estimates of the same equations, suggesting bias is not a serious problem in the latter.

In the present chapter, all equations are estimated for the postwar period as a whole. The data used, together with a description of how they were constructed and the original sources from which they were taken, are given in the appendix to this book.

## The Wage-Price-Profit Subsystem

The wage-change equation is now augmented with equations explaining profit rates and the change in profit rates in manufacturing, the rate of change in the cost of living, and the rate of change in the price of manufacturing output. Together, these equations form a wage-price-profit subsystem of the manufacturing sector of the economy.

Isolating these particular relations for estimation implies certain assumptions about the economy. In particular, it assumes that the dependent variables from the equations in the wage-price-profit subsystem have no important effect on the independent variables in the system. In the strict Walrasian conception of an interdependent economy, this assumption is incorrect. But as a practical matter, it is one that has to be made, and the only question is at what point to draw the line. In the present case, the important real quantity variables, output and employment, have been treated as autonomous and not explained by the subsystem, as have the prices of services, raw materials, and food.[1]

Including the original wage-change equation, there are four equations and an identity in the wage-price-profit subsystem. They are the following:

$$w_t = a_0 + a_1 c_{t-1} + a_2 U_t^{-1} + a_3 R_{t-1} + a_4 \Delta R_t + e_t \tag{5.1}$$

$$c_t = b_0 + b_1 {}^m p_{t-1} + b_2 {}^s p_t + b_3 {}' p_t + e_t \tag{5.2}$$

---

[1] There is, of course, no real division such as the one created here. In fact the quantity of manufactured products demanded, and hence output, will depend on prices in manufacturing; and the division of total income, and therefore probably real aggregate demand and unemployment, will depend on wage rates and prices. These effects are assumed small compared to the changes in output and employment resulting from other sources.

$$^mp_t = d_0 + d_1 w_t + d_2\,^rp_t + d_3\,\Delta(Q/K)_t + d_4\,(Q/K)_t + e_t \quad (5.3)$$

$$\Delta R_t = f_0 + f_1 w_{t-1} + f_2\,^rp_{t-1} + f_3\,^mp_t + f_4\,\Delta(Q/K)_t + e_t \quad (5.4)$$

$$R_t = R_{t-1} + \Delta R_t \quad (5.5)$$

The variables not previously used are defined as follows:

$^mp$  is the annual percentage change in (the index of) manufacturing output prices;

$^sp$  is the annual percentage change in the price of services to consumers;

$^fp$  is the annual percentage change in raw-food prices;

$^rp$  is the annual percentage change in the index of raw-material prices;

$(Q/K)$  is an index of capacity utilization in manufacturing averaged over the four quarters ending with the current quarter;

$\Delta(Q/K)$  is the quarterly change in the $(Q/K)$ index (hence an index of the change between the current quarter's capacity utilization rate and the rate a year earlier).

Changes in average labor productivity are not explicitly included in any of the equations. It is important to distinguish between the effect of trend productivity changes and changes in the output-per-labor-input ratio that result from firms operating at other than normal capacity levels. The implications of the latter on costs, prices, and profits are incorporated in the $(Q/K)$ and $\Delta(Q/K)$ variables. Trend productivity changes occur gradually and continuously, especially at the present level of aggregation, and are assumed to be adequately incorporated in the constant terms. This treatment is appropriate since the relevant dependent variables are all percentage rates of change. The impact of productivity changes, entering as just described, are discussed when the estimates of Equations 5.3 and 5.4 are interpreted later.

Equation 5.2 needs little explanation. The percentage changes in the prices of services, $^sp$, and raw food, $^fp$, enter directly into the percentage changes in the cost of of living, $c$, and so are included without lag. Raw-food prices are used rather than all foods in order to avoid any overlap with the index of output prices for manufacturing that would occur if processed foods were included. The index of output prices for manufacturing gives wholesale or factory prices. A lag of one quarter is therefore allowed for the effect of percentage changes in that index, $^m p$, to reach the cost of living as measured by the Consumer Price Index.

Equation 5.3 describes the percentage changes in manufacturing prices, $^m p$, according to a modified markup view of pricing. The variables $w$ and $^r p$ represent the percentage changes in the main direct-cost items: the average wage rate and the price of raw-material inputs into the manufacturing sector. The variable $\Delta(Q/K)$ is the change in the index of capacity utilization. It represents movements from one part of a typical cost curve to another. By comparison, changes in wages and raw-materials input prices represent shifts up or down of the cost curves. Implicit in the use of $\Delta(Q/K)$ as an explanatory variable is the presumption that average costs change with changes in the degree of capacity utilization, and that these changes are monotonic over the range of experience of the period studied. In particular, this formulation assumes that average costs fall as capacity utilization increases, so that a negative sign is expected for the coefficient of $\Delta(Q/K)$ in the equation for the change in output prices. The last term, $(Q/K)$, is the index of capacity utilization itself. Its role in this equation is entirely different from that of $\Delta(Q/K)$ just discussed. The relative pressure of demand is represented by $(Q/K)$. It modifies the effect of changes in unit costs, as reflected in the other three variables, in this otherwise purely cost-markup equation. The stronger the pressure on capacity, the larger will be the change in output prices resulting from any given change in unit costs. Because it reflects demand forces, $(Q/K)$ is expected to have a positive coefficient, as are $w$ and $^r p$.

Equation 5.4 describes the change in profit rate resulting from changes in variables reflecting unit costs, unit revenues, and volume. Since the purpose of this equation is to tie together the relevant variables of the present system, the profit equation is not specified in a definitional way. Instead it uses the variables in the form they have in the wage equation. For instance, rather than the total wage bill or wage costs per unit of output, the wage rate variable, $w$, from Equation 5.7 is used. The variables $w$ and $^r p$ are used to reflect cost changes. They are lagged one quarter because of the manufacturing time interval between the input of factors and the sale of the product. The effect of output price changes on profits is captured by $^m p$. and $\Delta(Q/K)$ reflects movements to more or less efficient levels of production and the effect of quantity changes on profits. According to their roles in this equation, negative coefficients would be expected for the first two variables and positive coefficients for the last two.

## Data Used

Before going on to the estimates of these equations for the post-war period, a few comments on the suitability of the data used are in order. The series used for the different variables are given in the appendix, together with an explanation of how they were constructed and what the sources of original data were. For all the variables except $(Q/K)$ and $\Delta(Q/K)$, suitable data were available to approximate closely the desired theoretical concepts. However, the $(Q/K)$ series is not as good as one would wish owing mainly to the denominator that is supposed to measure manufacturing capacity. The data actually used for $K$ are from the Department of Commerce series on deflated net value of structures and equipment in manufacturing. This series is not accurate for two main reasons. It reflects depreciation procedures rather than actual deterioration of productive capacity; and it is an annual series which had to be interpolated for use in the quarterly $(Q/K)$ series. Fortunately, movements in the numerator, $Q$, dominate the changes in $(Q/K)$, so the inadequacies of the $K$ series are minimized.

## The Equation Estimates

The least-squares estimates of the complete system, including the profit-rate identity, are as follows:

$$w_t = -4.313 + \underset{(0.054)}{0.367} c_{t-1} + \underset{(2.188)}{14.711} U_t{}^{-1} + \underset{(0.108)}{0.424} R_{t-1}$$
$$+ \underset{(0.172)}{0.792} \Delta R_t + e_t, \qquad R^2 = 0.870, \qquad (5.6)$$

$$c_t = -0.861 + \underset{(0.042)}{0.360}\,{}^m p_{t-1} + \underset{(0.135)}{0.599}\,{}^s p_t + \underset{(0.019)}{0.051}\,{}' p_t + e_t,$$
$$R^2 = 0.856, \qquad (5.7)$$

$${}^m p_t = -15.033 + \underset{(0.119)}{0.466}\, w_t + \underset{(0.023)}{0.344}\,{}^r p - \underset{(0.122)}{0.610}\, \Delta(Q/K)_t$$
$$+ \underset{(0.049)}{0.149}\,(Q/K)_t + e_t, \qquad R^2 = 0.921, \qquad (5.8)$$

$$\Delta R_t = 0.068 - \underset{(0.032)}{0.069\, w_{t-1}} - \underset{(0.011)}{0.036\, {}^r p_{t-1}} + \underset{(0.029)}{0.101\, {}^m p_t}$$

$$+ \underset{(0.033)}{0.248\, \Delta(Q/K)_t} + e_t, \qquad R^2 = 0.734, \qquad (5.9)$$

$$R_t = R_{t-1} + \Delta R_t. \tag{5.10}$$

Equation 5.6 is the same as Equation 3.8 from Chapter 3. It is given here and renumbered with the other equations for convenience. The implications of the other equations deserve some comment at this point.

### The Cost of Living

Equation 5.7 describes the annual cost-of-living change as a function of annual changes in other basic price series. Eighty-six percent of the variation in $c$ is explained by the regression. The negative constant term has no obvious interpretation. It may indicate something like a secular decline in percentage retail markups on manufactured products, which would show up in the constant term rather than the coefficient of ${}^m p$. It may also reflect the presence of some other component of the cost of living which is not included in the equation, although the terms that are included are sufficiently exhaustive that no obvious missing component comes to mind.

Apart from the constant term, the coefficients add to 1.01, indicating an elasticity of cost of living of virtually one to equal percentage increases in the other three price series. In the absence of whatever effects are incorporated in the constant term, an $x$ percent change in the series for the prices of crude foods, services, and manufacturing output lagged one quarter would lead to about an $x$ percent change in the cost of living.

### Manufacturing Prices

Equation 5.8 relates output price changes in manufacturing to changes in major determinants of cost and to the pressure of demand, in a modified markup theory of pricing. Ninety-two percent of the variation in ${}^m p$ is associated with the explanatory variables. The constant term in this equation should incorporate the effect of increases in labor productivity, but to interpret it one must first solve out the $(Q/K)$ term at its average value, which was 97.2 over the period covered. Multiplying this by the coefficient of

$(Q/K)$ reduces the constant term to —0.59. Thus the effect of productivity increases is to lower the output price, but by less than 1 percent annually. The balance of the benefits of productivity changes are used up in other ways, going into profits or being absorbed by cost increases in other parts of a firm's operations. Since increases in the average productivity of production workers are frequently associated with changes in operations that substitute an indirect cost for direct labor costs, the absorption of part of the productivity gain in these other costs is expected. Of course, the whole gain should not be absorbed in this way, since the reason for changing operations is presumably to achieve lower total costs. This puts an upper limit of zero on the constant term, while the lower limit is the full increase in productivity.[2] The estimate of —0.59 is easily within these limits.

All coefficients in Equation 5.8 are significant at the 0.99 probability level, and all have the anticipated sign. The elasticity of output prices to equal percentage changes in wage rates and raw-materials prices is 0.81, indicating some other inputs are present whose costs are not included in the variables $w$ and $^rp$. This is to be expected since these two variables take no account of indirect costs. The coefficient of $w$ is 0.466. This coefficient could be used to trace the direct circle from wages to prices to cost of living and back to wages again. By this route, an initial increase in wages will be reinforced two quarters later by another increase of 0.06 times the original one. But this is not the full circular effect since the same variables are also interrelated through profits. Discussion of the full effect must await the solution of the whole subsystem for its dynamic properties.

### Profit Rates

The last equation estimated is 5.9. It relates the change in profit rate to changes in wage rates, raw material prices, output prices, and the change in $(Q/K)$, reflecting both quantity produced and relative positions on cost curves. All variables have the expected coefficients and are significant at the 0.95 probability level. In interpreting the numerical estimates from this equation, one must remember that $\Delta R$ is only one fourth as large as the actual change

[2] This treatment assumes there is no secular change in the profit potential of the manufacturing sector resulting from institutional changes such as a tendency toward more monopoly control of prices. If such a tendency were present—say a persistent increase in prices despite constant total unit costs— it would be reflected in the constant term together with the effect of productivity changes, and the limits one could place on that term would change.

in profit rate over the four-quarter period that it represents. This follows from the definition of $R$ as a four-quarter average of profit rates, with $\Delta R$ as the quarterly first difference of this average.

With wages, raw material prices, output prices, and utilization rates all constant, Equation 5.9 reduces to $\Delta R = 0.068$. Four times this, or 0.27, is the annual increase in profit rate predicted by the equation as a result of historical productivity increases under these conditions. However, this estimate may be too low. With wage rates rising 3 percent a year and all prices and $(Q/K)$ constant, the equation predicts a decline in profit rates of over one half a percentage point each year. It is possible that the $(Q/K)$ series develops a slight bias over time as a measure of utilization rates. For instance, the first and last observations on $(Q/K)$ given in the data appendix show values of 100.0 for 1960-III and 98.0 for 1948-II. This despite an unemployment rate over 5 percent in 1960 and under 4 percent in 1948. If this reflects in part a distortion in the $(Q/K)$ index, maintaining constant utilization rates may correspond to a small rise in $(Q/K)$ over a year's time. If a correct adjustment factor were a rise of 0.1 percentage point per quarter in the $(Q/K)$ index, then full utilization and constant prices and wages would imply an annual rise in profit rates of 0.67 percentage points. A 3 percent annual increase in wage rates would now yield an annual decline of 0.16 percentage points in profit rates. A further adjustment may be needed to account for the liberalization of depreciation practices that has occurred over the postwar years. Such liberalization would probably show up in a reduced estimate of the constant term in Equation 5.9. Together with the adjustment in the $(Q/K)$ series suggested earlier, an increase in the constant term from 0.07 to 0.11 would now yield a prediction of constant profit rates when wage rates rose 3 percent a year and prices and utilization rates were unchanged. These same adjustments would now yield a predicted increase in profit rates of 0.8 percentage points each year with wage rates, prices, and utilization rates all constant. Such adjustments are only suggestive, and no attempt was made to re-estimate the equation with the raw data corrected along these lines.

## An Unlagged Variation of the Subsystem Equations

Equations 5.6 through 5.10 represent the preferred form of the wage-price-profit subsystem of equations. However, one alternative form of the equations is worth presenting as well; this is the case in which all time lags are removed from the variables in the preferred form. If these lags were, in fact, very short so that this alternative were a correct approximation, one would expect problems of simultaneous equations bias in least-squares estimates to be most prominent. Therefore, for this unlagged variation on the basic system, least-squares and two-stage least-squares estimates are computed and compared.

### Alternative Estimates and the Question of Bias

The alternative system of equations is given here and numbered 5.1′ through 5.5′.

$$w_t = a_0' + a_1'c_t + a_2'U^{-1} + a_3'R_t + a_4' \Delta R_t + e_t \tag{5.1′}$$

$$c_t = b_0' + b_1' {}^m p_t + b_2' {}^s p_t + b_3' {}^b p_t + e_t \tag{5.2′}$$

$$^m p_t = d_0' + d_1'w_t + d_2' {}^r p_t + d_3' \Delta(Q/K)_t + d_4' (Q/K)_t + e_t \tag{5.3′}$$

$$\Delta R_t = f_0' + f_1'w_t + f_2' {}^r p_t + f_3' {}^m p_t + f_4' \Delta(Q/K)_t + e_t \tag{5.4′}$$

$$R_t = R_{t-1} + \Delta R_t \tag{5.5′}$$

Since these equations form a nonrecursive system, coefficient estimates from least-squares regressions on the individual equations will be biased to an unknown degree. Estimates from two-stage least-squares regressions will be asymptotically unbiased. Although the properties of the latter estimates in small samples are not known, if they agree closely with the simple least-squares estimates, they offer what evidence there is that the problem of bias is not serious.

The coefficient estimates of Equations 5.1′ through 5.4′ using both two-stage least squares and simple least squares are compared in Table 5.1. Judged from the estimates given in this table, the amount of bias involved in the simple least-squares estimates is quite small. For almost every coefficient listed, the difference between the least squares and the asymptotically unbiased estimate shows up in the third, or at worst, the second, significant digit. The only exceptions are the constant and one other term in Equation 5.4′. This is the worst of the equations in the sense that using the unlagged form, Equation 5.4′, in place of the original Equation 5.4 seems to involve a significant specification error. Three of the coefficient estimates of Equation 5.4′ are insignificantly different from zero. This instability of the estimates when only minor changes are made in the lag structure may be a warning regarding the preferred profit equation as well. Further exploration of this relation is no doubt in order, and it should probably be considered the least certain of the relations in the subsystem presented here.

TABLE 5.1

A COMPARISON OF COEFFICIENT ESTIMATES USING SIMPLE
LEAST SQUARES AND TWO-STAGE LEAST SQUARES

| | Equation 5.1′ | | | | |
| --- | --- | --- | --- | --- | --- |
| | $a_0'$ | $a_1'$ | $a_2'$ | $a_3'$ | $a_4'$ |
| TSLS | − 4.565 | 0.355 | 16.146 | 0.420 | 0.552 |
| LS | − 4.562 | 0.342 | 16.045 | 0.424 | 0.472 |

| | Equation 5.2′ | | | |
| --- | --- | --- | --- | --- |
| | $b_0'$ | $b_1'$ | $b_2'$ | $b_3'$ |
| TSLS | − 1.470 | 0.312 | 0.816 | 0.071 |
| LS | − 1.448 | 0.350 | 0.788 | 0.065 |

| | Equation 5.3′ | | | | |
| --- | --- | --- | --- | --- | --- |
| | $d_0'$ | $d_1'$ | $d_2'$ | $d_3'$ | $d_4'$ |
| TSLS | − 15.495 | 0.440 | 0.346 | − 0.620 | 0.154 |
| LS | − 15.033 | 0.466 | 0.344 | − 0.610 | 0.149 |

| | Equation 5.4′ | | | | |
| --- | --- | --- | --- | --- | --- |
| | $f_0'$ | $f_1'$ | $f_2'$ | $f_3'$ | $f_4'$ |
| TSLS | 0.116 | − 0.014 | 0.057 | − 0.120 | 0.148 |
| LS | 0.053 | − 0.004 | 0.052 | − 0.110 | 0.158 |

## A Conjecture About Bias in the Preferred Equations

It is interesting that, except for the equations explaining profit rates, the coefficients in the unlagged equations are not much different from their counterparts in the preferred system presented earlier. This suggests the conjecture that the present evidence of the two-stage least-squares estimates regarding bias may carry over to the estimates of the preferred equations, 5.6 through 5.9.

Direct evidence that least-squares estimates for the preferred system are near consistent estimates would be useful, especially for the wage-change equation on which the results of Chapters 3 and 4 were based. In the present study, however, it was not possible to test this directly for reasons explained later. Instead, at the time the two-stage least-squares regressions were run on the unlagged system of equations, I hoped to prove formally that the implications of the Table 5.1 comparison carried over to least-squares estimates of the preferred system. However, I have not succeeded in this proof, and the connection remains only a conjecture.

The intuitive motivation for the conjecture rests on two points. The first is the similarity between the coefficient estimates in the preferred and unlagged forms of the equations in question. The second has to do with the way in which the question of possible bias arises in the preferred equations. This can be explained briefly with reference to the wage-change equation.

Owing to the four-quarter span of the dependent variable, the error terms in the wage equation are serially correlated. That up to third-order autocorrelation in the errors can be expected is shown analytically at the start of Chapter 3 when the wage equation is introduced. And that at least first-order autocorrelation in the errors is in fact present is evidenced by the value of 1.2 for the Durbin-Watson statistic for the final wage-change equation. If it were not for these autocorrelated errors, one could expect to get unbiased and efficient estimates using simple least squares on the wage-change equation. However, the presence of this autocorrelation raises what can be viewed as a modified form of simultaneous equations bias, despite the presence of lags in the system.

Consider a hypothetical system of two equations, where $v_t$ and $u_t$ are disturbance terms:

$$Y_t = aX_t + v_t$$

and

$$X_t = bY_{t-1} + cZ_t + u_t.$$

Under fairly simple assumptions, including the assumption that $v_t$ is uncorrelated with $X_t$, simple least squares will yield unbiased estimates in the first equation. But if $v_t$ is correlated with $v_{t-1}$, the assumption that $v_t$ is uncorrelated with $X_t$ will not hold. From the first equation, $v_{t-1}$ will be correlated with $Y_{t-1}$, and from the second, it will be correlated therefore with $X_t$. The bias in a least-squares estimate of $a$ in the first equation depends on the correlation between $v_t$ and $Y_{t-1}$, which in turn depends on the serial correlation in $v_t$. If the equations were truly simultaneous, $Y_{t-1}$ would be replaced by $Y_t$ in the second equation. And in this case, the place in the argument of the serial correlation relating $v_t$ and $v_{t-1}$ would be replaced, in effect, by the fact that $v_t$ is perfectly correlated with itself. Thus the bias that arises because $v_t$ is serially correlated appears to be modified from the true simultaneous equation problem to the extent the serial correlation of $v_t$ is less than perfect. And it is this apparent similarity that contributed to the conjecture that evidence on the unlagged system (true simultaneous equations) carried over to the preferred equations (modified simultaneous equations problem). However, this discussion suggests only the intuitive background for the conjecture, and the rigorous connection between the estimation properties in the two cases remains undiscovered and unproved.

This explanation of the way the bias question arises in the preferred system also suggests why it was not useful to employ the available two-stage least-squares estimation program on that system directly. The procedure of two-stage least squares is equivalent to the following: Estimates are first made of the reduced forms of the equations using simple least squares. In effect, the estimated values of the dependent variables from these first-stage regressions are then substituted for the corresponding explanatory variables whenever they appear in the structural equations, and the revised structural equations are estimated by simple least squares. The coefficients estimated in this second stage are the asymptotically unbiased, or consistent, two-stage least-squares estimates for the original structural equations.

The difficulty in using two-stage least squares to deal with the present case is evident from this description. In the wage-price-profit subsystem, the dependent variable of one equation appears as an explanatory variable in other equations, but generally with a one-quarter lag. There are no first-stage estimates of these lagged variables to use in the second stage. Therefore, the estimates would be no different from simple least-squares estimates for an equation such as the wage relation.

Further work on getting consistent estimates for a complete system of equations including a wage relation such as that developed here would be in order and might verify or modify the estimates that have been made. In the study by Klein and Ball,[3] least-squares estimates of a wage-change relation using unemployment and prices as explanatory variables were found insignificantly different from consistent estimates of the same relation, a finding that lends some support to the least-squares estimates used here.

[3] Klein, L. R., and R. J. Ball, "Some Econometrics of Determination of Absolute Prices and Wages," *Economic Journal*, Vol. 69 (September 1959).

## The Dynamic Properties of the Wage-Price-Profit Subsystem

In order to examine the interactions of the variables in the preferred subsystem presented earlier, Equations 5.1 through 5.5 must
must be solved simultaneously. Doing this will yield a difference
equation describing any one of the variables as a function of lagged
values of itself, plus lagged and unlagged values of the exogenous
variables of the system. This difference equation will embody all
the direct and indirect relations inherent in the original equations,
and will permit us to trace the effect over time of any initial impulse
given to the system. It will then be possible to see whether such
an impulse dies out quickly after its initial effect or whether its
effect is largely perpetuated or even reinforced by the interactions
of the system. The often mentioned wage-price spiral describes a
system in which initial shocks are perpetuated. The analysis will
show whether this description fits the present case.

Since wage-rate change is the variable of principal interest in this
study, the system is solved for the difference equation in $w_t$. However, the conclusions reached are not limited to the behavior of that
variable alone. Since the other dependent variables are all linearly
related to $w_t$, their dynamic characteristics will be essentially the
same.

Solving the Equations 5.1 through 5.5 yields a difference equation
in $w_t$ of the form

$$w_t = g_1 w_{t-1} + g_2 w_{t-2} + g_3 w_{t-3} + F_t. \tag{5.11}$$

The coefficients of the predetermined variables on the right are
functions of the coefficients of the explanatory variables in the
original Equations 5.1 through 5.5, and they are defined as follows:

$$g_1 = (1 - a_4 d_1 f_3 + a_3 f_3 d_1 + a_4 f_1) \left( \frac{1}{1 - a_4 d_1 f_3} \right), \tag{5.12a}$$

$$g_2 = (a_3 f_1 + a_1 b_1 d_1 - a_4 f_1) \left( \frac{1}{1 - a_4 d_1 f_3} \right), \tag{5.12b}$$

$$g_3 = (- a_1 b_1 d_1) \left( \frac{1}{1 - a_4 d_1 f_3} \right). \tag{5.12c}$$

The last term in Equation 5.11, $F_t$, is the forcing function. It is
a function of the coefficients, constant terms, and exogenous variables of the original equations, and it is defined as follows:

$$F_t = G_t - G_{t-1} + \left(\frac{a_3}{1 - a_4 d_1 f_3}\right)\Big[f_0 + d_0 f_3 + d_2 f_3\, {}^r p_{t-2}$$

$$+ f_2\, {}^r p_{t-3} + d_4 f_3\left(\frac{Q}{K}\right)_{t-2}$$

$$+ (d_2 f_3 + f_4)\,\Delta\left(\frac{Q}{K}\right)_{t-2}\Big], \quad (5.13)$$

where $G_t$ is defined as

$$G_t = \frac{1}{1 - a_4 d_1 f_3}\Big[a_0 + a_2 U_t^{-1} + a_1 b_0 + a_1 b_1\, {}^s p_{t-1} + a_1 b_3\, {}^f p_{t-1}$$

$$+ a_4 d_0 f_3 + a_4 d_2 f_3\, {}^r p_t + a_4 d_3 f_3\, \Delta\left(\frac{Q}{K}\right)_t + a_4 d_4 f_3\left(\frac{Q}{K}\right)_t$$

$$+ a_3 d_0 f_3 + a_3 d_2 f_3\, {}^r p_{t-1} + a_3 d_3 f_3\, \Delta\left(\frac{Q}{K}\right)_{t-1} + a_3 d_4 f_3\left(\frac{Q}{K}\right)_{t-1}$$

$$+ a_1 b_1 d_0 + a_1 b_1 d_2\, {}^r p_{t-2} + a_1 b_1 d_3\, \Delta\left(\frac{Q}{K}\right)_{t-2} + a_1 b_1 d_4\left(\frac{Q}{K}\right)_{t-2}$$

$$+ a_4 f_0 + a_4 f_2\, {}^r p_{t-2} + a_4 f_4\, \Delta\left(\frac{Q}{K}\right)_t + a_3 f_0 + a_3 f_2\, {}^r p_{t-2}$$

$$+ a_3 f_4\, \Delta\left(\frac{Q}{K}\right)_{t-1}\Big]. \quad (5.13a)$$

This general form is clearly unmanageable for most analytical purposes. However, the steady state case where all the variables in $F_t$ are at some constant value is a useful specific form for $F_t$ and is manageable. In this case, the expression of Equation 5.13 reduces to

$$F^* = \left(\frac{a_3}{1 - a_4 d_1 f_3}\right)\Big[f_0 + d_0 f_3 + d_4 f_3\left(\frac{Q}{K}\right)^*$$

$$+ (f_2 + d_2 f_3)\, {}^r p^*\Big] \quad (5.14)$$

where asterisks indicate a constant value for the variable through time.

Equation 5.11 is the general form of the difference equation in $w_t$. Dropping $F_t$ from the right side of that equation leaves the corresponding homogeneous equation, which can be solved to discover most of the independent dynamic characteristics inherent in the system. Further on, we will consider the problem of finding the general solution to the complete Equation 5.11, with a forcing function given by Equation 5.14.

### The Solution of the Homogeneous Equation

To solve the homogeneous form of Equation 5.11, it is necessary to find the characteristic roots of the corresponding characteristic equation,

$$q^3 = g_1 q^2 + g_2 q + g_3. \tag{5.15}$$

Solving this cubic equation with the estimated coefficient values given in Equations 5.6 through 5.9 yields the following characteristic roots (where $i = \sqrt{-1}$):

$q_1 = 0.940,$
$q_2 = 0.012 + 0.261i,$
$q_3 = 0.012 - 0.261i.$

The solution of the homogeneous equation is therefore

$$w_t = k_1(0.940)^t + k_2(0.012 + 0.261i)^t + k_3(0.012 - 0.261i)^t, \tag{5.16}$$

which reduces to the equivalent form

$$w_t = k_1(0.940)^t + (0.261)^t (k_4 \cos 1.53t + k_5 \sin 1.53t). \tag{5.17}$$

The constants $k_1$, $k_4$, and $k_5$ must be evaluated with a particular solution and are left undetermined for the present.

Both terms on the right side of Equation 5.17 contain numbers smaller than one raised to the power $t$, so the behavior of $w_t$ is eventually to damp out any initial movement. The first term on the right side provides a trend component to the path of $w_t$ over time, the trend going exponentially from $k_1$ to zero after any initial shock. The second term adds an oscillatory component to the path of $w_t$, with the amplitude of the oscillations damping to zero with time. The system described by Equation 5.17 can therefore be characterized as one of damped oscillations along an exponential trend approaching zero. Since $w_t$ is the rate of change of the wage level, $w_t$ approaching zero from some positive number means wage rates are rising, but at a decreasing rate.

Without evaluating the constants, one cannot be certain about the relative roles of the two terms or the absolute effect of either. But assuming, to start, that the constants are not such as to make either term negligible, some description can be made.

The trend term contains 0.940 raised to the power $t$, so that its rate of damping will be slow. Through this term, an initial impulse will have a noticeable effect on $w$ for several periods. For example, one year, $t = 4$, after a once-and-for-all shock from the forcing function $w$, will still be augmented by about $0.78k_1$ from this term.

By contrast, the amplitude of the cyclical term includes 0.261 raised to the $t$ power so that its effect will die out rapidly. After one year, the amplitude of the fluctuations will be only about 0.005 times their original size. Equation 5.17 also shows the period of the cycle is 4.1, indicating this many quarters are required for the cyclical term to repeat itself. With the previous calculation of the amount of damping after four quarters, this shows successive cycles will have an amplitude of only 0.005 times the preceding one. After a short time, just a quarter or two, the cyclical component of the path of $w$ will be negligible even with a large initial amplitude.

### A General Solution

To explore the characteristics of the system further, the general solution to Equation 5.11 can be found. To do this, it is necessary to find a particular solution satisfying that equation and add it to the solution of the homogeneous equation given by Equation 5.17. The constants $k_1$, $k_4$, and $k_5$ can then be evaluated from a set of initial conditions. Since the solution thus obtained will depend on the form assumed for the forcing function and since, in turn, this form will only approximate the true observations used in evaluating the particular solution, the results are only illustrative and do not have the same general significance as the rest of the discussion.

The only manageable possibility for a particular solution is the solution for a steady state with a constant forcing function. In this case, the forcing function is given by Equation 5.14, and the steady-state case described by

$$w^* = (g_1 + g_2 + g_3) w^* + F^* \tag{5.18}$$

reduces to

$$w^* = \frac{-f_0 - d_0 f_3 - (f_2 + d_2 f_3)\,{}^r p^* - d_4 f_3 (Q/K)^*}{f_1 + d_1 f_3} \tag{5.19}$$

after substituting for $g_1$, $g_2$, $g_3$, and $F^*$ in terms of the variables and coefficients of the original equations. It is interesting and somewhat surprising that Equation 5.19 shows the steady-state value of $w$ to depend directly on only two of the autonomous variables, $^rp$ and $(Q/K)$. The others are eliminated in the interrelationships of the five equations when the steady-state condition is imposed.

Equation 5.19 can be solved for any constant values of the variables on the right, and is now solved for $(Q/K)^* = 102.5$ and $^rp = 1.33$. This value for raw-materials prices is the mean for the period of this study. The value 102.5 can be considered as a target for the index of capacity utilization, although it is not a maximum since higher figures were recorded occasionally in the period. This particular value was chosen for reasons connected with evaluating the general solution, which will be made clear later. The value of $w^*$ resulting from these steady-state conditions is 3.98 percent per year.

The general solution of the original difference equation is now of the form

$$w_t = k_1(0.940)^t + (0.261)^t (k_4 \cos 1.53t + k_5 \sin 1.53t) + 3.98,$$

$$(5.20)$$

where the particular solution has been added to Equation 5.17. It remains to evaluate the constants, $k_1$, $k_4$, and $k_5$. To do this, the three quarters starting with the fourth quarter of 1955 were used as initial conditions. These were chosen for two reasons. The first is the good fit of the estimating equation for wages in this period, as reflected in the relatively small residuals for the three quarters.[4] The second is that the value of $(Q/K)$ reaches a new level in the first of these quarters about equal to its value used in getting the particular solution, and then remains virtually constant.[5] Starting with the fourth quarter of 1955, $(Q/K)$ is 102.5, 102.7, and 102.1. This allows evaluation of the general solution of the difference equation under conditions that are approximately appropriate to the particular solution used. Ideally, we would like a controlled experiment in which the forcing function moved to a constant level and stayed there. In fact, the actual system is subject to repeated shocks from an ever changing forcing function. The best we can do to solve the difference equation analytically is to pick a period when the conditions of the controlled experiment are at least approximated. The period was chosen in an attempt to do this.

---

[4] The residuals were —0.19, 0.06, 0.83.
[5] The effect of $^rp$ in Equation 5.19 is very small compared to that of $(Q/K)$.

Using the $w_t$ values for the three quarters chosen gives the following initial conditions:

$$w_0 = 4.52,$$
$$w_1 = 5.06,$$
$$w_2 = 5.56. \tag{5.21}$$

And using these in Equation 5.20 results in three equations for the three unknowns, $k_1$, $k_4$, and $k_5$. Solving these gives

$$k_1 = 1.71,$$
$$k_4 = -1.17,$$
$$k_5 = -1.98; \tag{5.22}$$

and the general solution is now

$$w_t = 1.71(0.940)^t + (0.261)^t (-1.17 \cos 1.53t \\ -1.98 \sin 1.53t) + 3.98. \tag{5.23}$$

The earlier observation that the oscillatory part of the solution very soon became negligible is not affected by these estimates of the constants since they are of moderate size. For $t$ equal to 1, 2, 3, and 4, the total contributions of the oscillatory part of the solution are $+0.483$, $+0.082$, $-0.036$, and $-0.007$ respectively. After one quarter, this component is important: it is still significant after the second and third; and it is just noticeable after the fourth. In effect, its main impact in this case is just to accelerate the damping of the total solution in the early quarters.

The evaluation of the constant in the trend term is more critical. This term alone damps slowly and so keeps contributing a large percentage of the value of its constant for several periods. If the constant is very small, this slow damping is of little importance. If it is very large, it will dominate the time sequence of $w$ for a long time because of the slow damping. In the present estimate, the constant is at neither of these extremes. It is of moderate size, $+1.71$, compared to the value of the forcing function. For $t$ equal to 1, 2, and 3, the contributions of this trend component in the solution are $+1.609$, $+1.513$, and $+1.341$. At $t = 10$, this component is still about $+0.5$.

One consequence of this slow damping of the trend component is that one can never expect to observe steady-state values of $w$. The period chosen for evaluating the general solution was one of unusual stability in the forcing function. Even so, $(Q/K)$ was approximately constant for only five periods. At the end of that time, the predicted $w$ was still far from its stationary solution value of 3.98. The cyclical term was nearly damped out, but the trend term was still $+1.34$ and the predicted $w$ was 5.38. Actual $w$ for that quarter was 5.95.

During almost all of the postwar period, as with most any period one might have observed, the forcing function actually has changed before even the cyclical term has damped out. Under such conditions, the observations of $w$ may be quite different from what would have been steady-state values under average, but constant, values of the forcing function.

A similar problem arises from the stochastic nature of the individual equations. This feature was ignored in solving the difference equation for wage changes. The presence of random disturbance terms in the original equations makes the solution of the system a random variable and precludes a complete description of its dynamic properties by analytical techniques. Simulation methods in which random disturbances are introduced offer the best means of examining the responses of the system, but these were beyond the scope of the present study. However, in a recent study by Duesenberry, Eckstein, and Fromm,[6] those authors did perform such experiments on an estimated macroeconomic model and concluded that the basic dynamic properties of their system, such as its damping characteristics, were not greatly changed by the introduction of appropriate random disturbances. Since the cyclical tendencies in the present system are so strongly damped, it is assumed that fluctuations arising from the stochastic element would be minor. However, further investigation using simulation techniques would be desirable.

[6] Duesenberry, James B., Otto Eckstein and Gary Fromm, " A Stimulation of the United States Economy in Recession," *Econometrica,* Vol. 28 (October 1960).

# 6

# Results, Implications, and Policies

## The Problem and the Basic Findings Relating to It

The results described up to now have a direct relevance for economic policy. Much of recent experience in the United States and elsewhere has pointed up the difficulty of simultaneously achieving low levels of unemployment and maintaining a stable general price level. In this country, the later years of the Eisenhower Administration were characterized by the acceptance of high unemployment as an alternative to any inflationary pressures at all. The Kennedy and Johnson Administrations have appeared unwilling to accept this high cost in unemployment and lost output. But while taking some significant expansionary steps, they have at the same time been confronted with difficulties in the nation's balance of international payments that have magnified the pressures for deflationary policies. In this environment, it is important to understand the nature of the choices open to policy. Both the immediate problem of choosing wisely and the further goal of improving the available choices depend on such understanding.

In this final chapter, the findings developed in the preceding chapters will be brought to bear on questions of policy. The main results of the analysis will be discussed in the light of their implications for some specific courses of action.

The factors affecting wage changes have been analyzed on the assumption that the wage relation is central to an understanding of the inflation problem. The levels of unemployment and profit rates and changes in living costs and profit rates (or unemployment) have been identified as important determinants of wage changes. Attention has focused on the wage change-unemployment relation since it is the choice between unemployment and inflation that poses the basic problems for policy. But explicit recognition has been given to the way in which this relation shifts with changes in the other determinants of wages.

Most of the quantitative findings have been based on the wage-change relation alone, with the productivity arithmetic used to link wage changes and inflation in a way that constituted an abbreviated general-equilibrium solution for wage behavior. The additional relations in the wage-price-profit subsystem of Chapter 5 served mainly to confirm the stability of the system implied in the calculations made on the wage equation, and to give some description of the nature of the dynamic process of adjustment. This relative emphasis on the wage-change equation alone will continue in the present chapter since a full analysis of all the relations involved in the inflation question is beyond the scope of the study. If one takes the view that price behavior is largely cost determined, at least in the manufacturing sector, then discussion from the wage-change equation alone omits little except for questions of speed of adjustment. On the other hand, if the inflation question is thought to depend only in small part on the behavior of wages, then the present results must be viewed as merely a start toward a full explanation.

### The Quantitative Results Generalized

The principal moral of the results developed here is that we have a mildly inflation-prone economy. The structure of the wage-determination processes is such that with low unemployment levels and with profit rates and productivity gains typical of postwar experience, wage changes will be inflationary. This conclusion holds using different estimates and allowing for considerable error. Table 6.1 summarizes the results implicit in the estimated wage-change relation; in particular, it shows the tolerable profit rates for combinations of unemployment and inflation when productivity growth proceeds at the historical 3 percent annual rate and constant income shares are assumed.

Since, without deliberate action to the contrary, high profit rates are typically associated with low unemployment rates, Table 6.1 does show that some inflation will have to be tolerated in operating the present economy at low levels of unemployment. It also shows that the degree of inflation that must be tolerated appears to be moderate, even without specific policies to alter the existing relationships: for instance, 4 percent unemployment is consistent with a 2 percent rate of inflation if profit rates are at 11.6 percent and pricing behavior follows the assumptions of the productivity arithmetic.

To do still better, two kinds of policy action suggest themselves. The first is to alter the historically typical relationships among the explanatory variables or to affect factors in the link between wage changes and inflation. In particular, it may be possible to keep profit rates moderate even though unemployment reaches low levels; or productivity growth may be accelerated so that less in-

TABLE 6.1

MANUFACTURING PROFIT RATES ASSOCIATED WITH VARIOUS
UNEMPLOYMENT RATES AND RATES OF INFLATION
(3 percent rate of productivity growth assumed) *

| Inflation Rate | Unemployment Rate (percent) | | | | |
|---|---|---|---|---|---|
| (percent per year) | 3.0 | 4.0 | 5.0 | 6.0 | |
| 0.0 | 5.7 | 8.6 | 10.3 | 11.5 | |
| 1.0 | 7.2 | 10.1 | 11.8 | 13.0 | Associated |
| 2.0 | 8.7 | 11.6 | 13.3 | 14.4 | Manufacturing |
| 3.0 | 11.7 | 14.6 | 16.3 | 17.4 | Profit Rates |

* Calculations are based on Equation 3.15, the central case which assumes unchanging income distribution, labor force distribution, and appropriate relative price shifts, with wages in all sectors of the economy changing at the same rate as those in manufacturing. The kinds of changes introduced by relaxing some of these assumptions were discussed at the end of Chapter 3.

flation is consistent with any given rate of wage increase. Specific policies that might serve these ends are considered later in this chapter. While some of them are ambiguous in their total effect and often have undesirable or at least unpredictable side effects, others seem more promising and suggest that policies can be successful in this area. The second possibility is to change the structure behind the wage equation so that less rapid wage increases are associated with any given set of values for the determinants of wage change. Drastic institutional changes are beyond the scope of practical policy proposals, but some shifting of the wage equation's parameters may be possible within the limits of moderate action. Before specific policy actions of either the first or second sort, are considered, the findings on each of the important explanatory factors will be reviewed.

*Unemployment*

The unemployment rate was found to have an important independent effect in determining wage changes throughout the postwar period. A linear relation between unemployment and wage changes was specifically rejected in favor of one which grows progressively steeper as lower unemployment levels are reached. As a result of this property, the change in the rate of wage increase, for example, is less than half as large for an unemployment change from 6 percent to 5 percent as for a change in unemployment from 4 percent to 3 percent.

Observations of extreme unemployment rates were not available in the postwar period so that extrapolation of this relation to very low unemployment is risky. If anything, there is evidence that with present institutions, a constraint of some kind is present that eventually limits the rate of wage increase. But this constraint, if present at all, begins to operate at very high rates of wage increase, probably above 10 percent per year. The area of main importance for policy is well short of this.

The increasing steepness of the unemployment curve over the generally experienced range of unemployment rates immdiately points to the need for countercyclical policies. Over a period of time, wage changes will be less for any given average unemployment level as the variation of unemployment around this average decreases. For example, with the unemployment form estimated, if unemployment alternates between 2.5 and 7.5 percent — a strong cyclical pattern averaging 5.0 percent unemployment — the annual rate of wage change will be nearly 1 percentage point higher than if a steady 5.0 percent unemployment rate were maintained throughout (assuming the other factors affecting wage changes were identical in both cases). The acceleration in wages that occurs between 5.0 and 2.5 percent unemployment is significantly greater than the deceleration that occurs between 5.0 and 7.5 percent.[1]

There are further gains likely from stability, which are dis-

---

[1] If Equation 3.8 is used, the difference in wage change resulting from 2.5 rather than 5.0 percent unemployment would be 14.711 [(1/2.5) —(1/5.0)] or 2.94 percent per year. The difference between 5.0 and 7.5 percent unemployment would be 14.711 [(1/5.0) —(1/7.5)] or 0.99 percent per year. Thus, if the time spent in transition is treated as negligible, wage increases in the cyclical case would be greater by 2.94 percent half the time and smaller by only 0.99 percent the other half.

cussed later. The preceding illustration shows only the effects inherent in the unemployment term itself. Using a different form for the unemployment term would give somewhat different quantitative results, but the principle remains as long as there is curvature within the range of variation of the unemployment rate.

### Cost of Living

The positive partial correlation observed between changes in living costs and subsequent changes in wages confirms the expectations for this relation. Furthermore, the results for different periods reflect the increased importance of cost-of-living clauses in the post-1953 period. And the separate equations estimated for the different subgroups suggest that living costs are somewhat more important in wage changes of durable-goods industries than in nondurables.

Wage increases have some feedback to further wage increases via cost-of-living effects. But the importance of this circular pattern should not be exaggerated. The elasticity of wages to living costs in the wage-change equation estimated for the entire postwar period is about one third. Taken together with a below-unity elasticity of living costs to wages, the circular effect from this source alone is seen to die out quickly. Even with an elasticity of wages to living costs of two thirds as estimated in the post-1953 equation, this effect is still moderate. Finally, taking account of all interactions through solution of the full wage-price-profit subsystem yields the same conclusion. The dynamic properties of that solution are such as to damp out an initial disturbance after some periods. The circular process whereby prices affect wages which in turn affect prices and profits (negatively) gives some appearance of a wage-price spiral, but one that disappears rather than becoming explosive or indefinitely self-perpetuating.

But although the interplay of wage and price changes does not yield the exaggerated spiral sometimes supposed, neither is it negligible. Policies to hold down elements of living costs not sensitive to wage changes, such as prices of imports and agricultural products, can be important in restraining wage increases and hence prices of wage-sensitive components of living costs. Similarly, it is important to restrain price behavior in oligopolistic industries, which have a good deal of discretion in fixing their markup over costs. But the effects here may come back on wages mainly through enhanced profits rather than increased living costs.

*Profit Rates*

Profits enter the inflation problem at two distinct points. First, in the product market, profits are the goal of pricing policies. Price increases may be initiated to restore profit margins (or maximize profits) in the face of cost increases; or may be initiated to augment (or maximize) profits independently of cost changes. Second, in the labor market, profit rates have been identified as a major determinant of wage changes.

This interrelationship in which profits both affect and are affected by wage changes gives rise to a range of possible explanations of inflationary phenomena. Wage increases that raise unit costs will initially reduce profit margins which may be restored, at least in part, through price increases. This is a standard wage-push argument. Alternatively, an initial attempt to raise profit rates through higher prices will lead to accelerated wage increases which then in turn may be passed forward into still higher prices if the higher profit rates are to be maintained. Or the same sequence can arise through an initial rise in profit rates stemming from exceptional productivity gains with no reduction in prices. In some circumstances, these could properly be labeled instances of profit-push inflation. The 1955–1958 wage and price rises in the United States may be in part a case of this kind.

In this study, the relation between profit rates and wage changes has been treated as a linear one. Alternative forms were not tried, but there is some evidence to suggest that the impact of profits may be magnified as larger profit rates are experienced. The main evidence on this point is the lower coefficient estimated for profit rates in the post-1953 wage equation compared to that for the earlier post-war years. The higher slope estimated for the earlier years is associated with observations of high profit rates, while the lower slope estimate accompanies relatively low profit rates. A nonlinear form might have accommodated both periods in a single estimate. The implication of this alternative is readily appended to the conclusions reached for the linear case. The main effect would be to amplify the importance of limiting cyclical variations in the economy. The consequences of the nonlinearity in the unemployment term in this respect were noted previously. If the effect of profit rates on wage changes were progressively greater as profit rates rose, the same implications would apply to this term also. Since profits vary sharply over a business cycle, over a period of time,

a given average profit rate would be less inflationary the less cyclical variation there were in the economy.

The direct impact of profit rates on wage changes is seen from the
wage-change equation. With the linear forms that were used, a
change in profit rates from a level of 10 percent to a new level of
11 percent would in itself raise the equilibrium rate of wage change
about 0.4 percent. This effect is about the same using either the
post-1953 or the postwar equation. (A nonlinear form for the
profit variable would call for a somewhat larger effect on wages
when profit rates were very high.) If price increases then followed
the higher wages in an attempt to maintain the new profit rates,
still higher wages would result.

On the basis of the assumptions outlined in Chapter 3, for any
assumed rate of productivity increase, the rate of price change can
be calculated as the difference between the rates of change in wages
and productivity. And with the relation, price changes can be solved
out of the wage relation, yielding a family of curves connecting
rates of wage and price change on the one hand with unemployment rates on the other, each curve being associated with a different
prevailing profit rate. Figures 3.8a, 3.8b, 3.8c, and 3.8d depicted
this family of curves for four different rates of productivity gain.
At successively higher profit rates, higher unemployment is needed
to hold wage changes and inflation at any given level.

Table 6.1 showed a range of profit rate, unemployment, and inflation combinations that are potentially available for policy choices
with the historic 3 percent rate of productivity increase. The quantitative importance of profits in affecting the inflation-unemployment trade-off is evident from the figures in that table. For example,
it shows that if 2 percent inflation is tolerated, a 4.0 percent unemployment rate is attainable with profit rates at 11.6 percent; but
only 5.0 percent unemployment can be attained if inflation is to
be held at this 2 percent rate while profit rates are at 13.3 percent.
A similar pattern prevails between profit rates and the attainable
unemployment rate at each level of inflation. Of course, as less inflation is tolerated, the restrictions imposed on the other variables
become more severe, and allowable profit rates are lower for any
given unemployment rate.

The separate equations estimated for the different subgroups
suggest that a given difference in profits has a somewhat greater
effect on wage changes in nondurable-goods industries than in

durables. However, in terms of explaining the observed movements in wages, this fact is offset by the greater cyclical variability of profits in durable-goods industries.

## Policies Not Altering the Wage Equation

On the basis of the estimated wage-change equation and the institutional structure underlying it, what policies might improve the estimated trade-off between inflation and unemployment? Several possibilities exist, although their ultimate impact is frequently uncertain, even as to the direction of the effect on the inflation question. Most of these policies divide into those that attempt to reduce profits at any given unemployment rate and those that attempt to accelerate productivity. The uncertainty about their ultimate effects stems in part from the fact that steps that appear to accomplish one of these goals often also appear to work adversely on the other.

### Changing the Corporate Tax Rate

Perhaps the most direct way of affecting profit rates is by changing the basic tax on corporate earnings, but this may also be the least desirable course for other reasons. The present tax structure involves important issues of equity among different taxpaying groups and incentive effects to private investment. Undesirable results on either score may outweigh whatever favorable results there are on the inflation issues. And even the favorable results are hard to gauge.

The unsettled question of the incidence of corporate taxes poses special questions. To the extent that a tax increase designed to lower profit rates were passed forward in the form of higher prices, the ultimate goal of price stability would be at least partially defeated. This is true directly because of the initially higher prices and indirectly because these, and the consequent less than full reduction in profit rates, lead to larger wage increases than would occur if none of the tax was passed forward.

On the other hand, to the extent that the incidence of higher taxes remains on profit rates, investment spending may be impaired. If, as one would expect, this restricts the growth of labor productivity, a given rate of wage increase becomes more inflationary at the same time that the real growth of output and incomes is restrained.

The Revenue Act of 1964 reduced most corporate tax rates by about 8 percent and by far more than this for small corporations. One would expect this to lead to a more rapid rate of wage increase as after-tax profit rates, at least initially, get the full benefit of tax reduction. Ultimately, the incidence of the reductions may in part or in full shift away from profit rates. And also in the longer run, whatever stimulation of investment occurs as a result of the tax change should accelerate productivity. Although the increased investment spending and other induced output changes will lower unemployment, thus indirectly causing more rapid wage increases from this source as well, this part of the response is common to any expansionary measure.

### Accelerated Depreciation

A different measure for affecting the stated profit rates of industry without directly altering its operation or structure is to adjust the depreciation methods permitted for tax purposes. In particular, a program of accelerated depreciation has the effect of postponing *stated* profits and of decreasing *stated* profits permanently as long as firms continue to expand their capital stock through net investment. And in contrast to raising the corporate tax rate, the great advantage of accelerated depreciation is that it also serves the goals of productivity increase and economic growth by stimulating investment through the postponement of tax liabilities on the returns to investment. In the present context, its main drawback is that it may not have the desired result on wage behavior. This would be so if, at the bargaining table, the new *stated* profit figures were not considered comparable with previous figures based on slower write-offs. In this case, the response of wages to profit rates might adjust to approximately what it would have been in the absence of accelerated depreciation. Indeed, the adjustment may go even further, with wages rising faster to capture a part of the tax advantage that is intended to encourage investment.

The net result on the wage question remains in doubt. But this in no way detracts from the appeal of accelerated depreciation on the other grounds mentioned: the encouragement of investment and hence stimulation of productivity growth. Although some measures may have little value for shifting the wage change-unemployment schedule by affecting profit rates, they may have an equivalent impact for price stability by raising the rate of productivity increase. Moreover in a choice between gaining price stability by lowering the rate of wage change or by raising the rate of productivity increase, the latter is clearly preferable. With prices stable in either instance, the faster increase of wages in the latter case means a faster growth of real incomes and living standards for wage earners, together with a corresponding faster growth of nonwage incomes.

In 1962, the Treasury Department prepared a broad revision of the *Bulletin F* schedule, which specifies the time over which assets may be depreciated for tax purposes. The revisions were almost without exception in the direction of permitting faster write-offs, so that in effect this allowed accelerated depreciation by comparison with the previous schedule. It will be difficult to tell whether the stated reduction in profits has any impact on wage changes, and certainly still too early to judge.

Further exploration of the way in which profit rates enter the wage relation should attempt to clarify the role of depreciation. It would be useful to see whether after-tax cash flow as a percentage of stockholders' equity explains wage changes better than the profit rate variable used here. It is difficult to make an *a priori* case clearly favoring either variable since, over some periods, an increase in cash flow relative to profits reflects a true increase in capital depreciation, while at other times it reflects only a change in accounting procedures. Ideally, one should use a concept that yielded cash flows over the entire period on a uniform accounting method that accurately reflected capital changes. The actual data available are far from this ideal, and an attempt to revise them to such a consistent basis is beyond the scope of this study.

*Other Tax Incentives*

In addition to accelerated depreciation, other tax changes may be employed to stimulate investment. One main alternative is a tax credit. Most simply, this scheme allows some part of capital investment expenditures to be subtracted from tax liabilities as the expenditures occur; depreciation then proceeds normally. By extending benefits only when investment takes place, such a program offers a larger investment incentive per dollar of tax revenue lost to the government, and for this reason it is a more efficient means of stimulating capital formation. On the other hand, it has a disadvantage for wage behavior since it results in a clear gain in after-tax profit rates, at least initially. On balance, the inflationary impact of the program depends on whether the resulting increase in productivity growth outweighs the upward pressure of higher profit rates on wage changes.

A bill providing for a tax credit on new investment in equipment was passed in 1962. The estimated initial increase in aggregate after-tax profits resulting from this bill was about 4 percent. Using Equation 3.8, this large a percentage change in profit rates would increase the annual rate of wage change by about 0.15 to 0.2 percentage points from the profit-rate term alone and, initially, by half again this much from the term for the change in profit rates. Thus, initially at least, the impact of such a measure on wage changes is substantial.

Some combination of increased corporate tax rates and specific tax incentives to investment could be used. Conceivably, such a combination could yield a net reduction in profit rates without impairing investment in the aggregate or perhaps even while providing a net inducement to investment spending.

### Domestic Policies To Foster Competition

Average profit rates vary widely among manufacturing industries and between the manufacturing sector and other parts of the economy. Higher average profit rates over time may be needed to compensate for the greater variability in profits in some industries. Nonetheless, there exists a presumption that striking and persistent profit-rate differentials may also reflect the ability to control prices in product markets. Where this is the case, the public interest would be served by increasing competition or competitive-like behavior. But this has always been acknowledged on other grounds, and the present findings only add a further consideration to the issue. Reducing profit rates everywhere to competitive levels should have the desirable effect of moderating wage increases. Yet in view of the myriad considerations involved in dealing with any industry's organizational structure, this result probably adds little for guiding proper policy in this area.

### Trade Policy To Foster Competition

While recent problems with the balance of international payments emphasize the desirability of price stability, freer trade offers one of the promising roads to a simultaneously more prosperous and less inflationary economy. The most direct effect of lowering trade barriers would be generally lower prices. Although harder to isolate and evaluate, a parallel benefit would be expected from increased aggregate productivity.

The impact of freer trade on price stability would come from several directions. By reducing the costs of imports, it would directly lower prices of consumer goods imported; simultaneously, it would increase competitive pressure on the prices of domestic consumer goods that are import competing. In the same way, intermediate goods and raw materials that are imported would be available at lower costs and would in turn exert competitive pressures on the prices of competing domestic products. And finally, the lower costs of all these goods would be reflected in the prices of the final products that utilize them as inputs.

The impact of increased competition would not end with the initial effects on prices. If foreign competition resulted in lower average profit rates, wage increases would be moderated for given levels of the other variables affecting wages. Thus the impact of freer trade on the wage change-unemployment relation would come both from pressure on consumer prices and from pressures on profit rates in any industries that might currently be enjoying a measure of monopoly profits because of tariff protection.

### A Stable, High-Level Economy as a Tool Against Inflation

In the longer run, perhaps the most important step toward achieving reasonable price stability together with low unemployment lies in actually reaching *and then maintaining* a high level of utilization of the nation's productive capacity. Although at any point in time, the problem is one of choosing between lower unemployment and more inflation, over a period of time the issue becomes that of shifting the terms on which this choice must be made. *Maintaining*, as opposed to reaching, low unemployment levels should help to shift this schedule in a desirable direction; while tolerating large cyclical movements, especially around a high unemployment mean, should have the opposite effect. This is true, somewhat incidentally, because policies such as those described which contain profit rates are more likely to succeed in a prosperous environment. A policy on profit rates must aim at shifting the aggregate relation between these rates and unemployment. To do so while at a low point on the schedule means putting pressure on profit rates that are already low. The resistance to specific policies may be greatest under such conditions and so may possible inequities. But in addition to this consideration, there exists a more direct and important case for low-unemployment policies.

During most of the postwar period, the American economy had been characterized by frequent cyclical swings around successively higher mean unemployment rates. A long-run condition of this sort results in profit-rate adjustments such that returns are satisfactory — or in equilibrium with the cost of capital — *over the average cycle.* Since profit rates vary cyclically, they are very high at the peak of the cycle when full employment exists. And these high profit rates then accelerate the rates of wage increase and hence the inflation that accompanies low unemployment. If low unemployment were a permanent condition, the profit rates associated with it would be reduced; and hence the accompanying rates of wage increase and inflation would be moderated.

To take an extreme case, assume the supply of equity capital is perfectly elastic at a 10 percent rate of return. Then profit rates would be no higher in a persistently tight economy than in a persistently soft one, being 10 percent in each case.

Now, with the same supply conditions, assume economic activity and profit rates vary cyclically. Profit rates will average 10 percent over a cycle. But at full-employment peaks they will be far in excess of this. Compared with the persistently tight economy described in the previous paragraph, full employment will be associated with higher profit rates and hence more rapid wage and price increases.

Relaxing the simple assumption made about the supply of capital should not alter this result in any important way. Let the supply of equity capital at any given level of income be less than perfectly elastic. Then if income were the same in either case and the steady full-employment economy required higher investment levels over a period of time, the investment would be associated with a higher cost of capital and average rates of return than in the cyclical case. But since income would be higher with steady full employment, therefore so would saving; and the supply of capital would be greater at each rate of return. On balance, the cost of capital might average higher or lower in this situation compared with the cyclical case, depending on which effect dominated. But even on the assumption that profit rates over a period of time would be somewhat higher with steady full employment, *at low unemployment* they would be lower if this were the persistent condition of the economy rather than a cyclical peak.

Actually other considerations support the view that over time the cost of capital might be lower with steady full employment. The terms on which capital is supplied make allowance for expected risk. Expected risk would probably be lower if the expected variability of the returns to capital were decreased. And the variability of returns from all investments would eventually be reduced in an environment of steady full employment.

These arguments have been in terms of shifting the inflation-unemployment relation by shifting the profit rate-unemployment relation. But maintaining a steady unemployment rate should improve the inflation problem directly as well. In the earlier discussion of the unemployment term in the wage relation, it was pointed out that the nonlinear form of the unemployment term made any steady unemployment rate less inflationary than the same rate when it was the average of cyclical variations in unemployment. And in addition to such an effect, the often made assumption that prices are less flexible downward than upward, if true, would reinforce such a result.

### Altering the Structure of the Wage Equation

Up to now, the discussion has been mainly of possibilities for acting on the explanatory variables in the wage equation. Improvement may also be possible through changes in the way that wages respond to *given* values of the explanatory variables.

Underlying the particular form of the estimated wage equation is the structure of the wage-determining institutions: the strength of labor and employer groups and the interactions between them. Demand forces are clearly evident in the explanatory variables; and the form of the equation may be interpreted as showing noncompetitive wage setting and therefore the presence of "push" forces of some kind. The findings are consistent with theories of inflationary bursts originating either with labor or nonlabor elements, and they are equally compatible with explanations in which demand forces are most prominent. But these matters are wedded together in the equation and not subject to clear distinction. In this, the formulation corresponds to the realities of the situation.

#### Institutional Changes

Since the structure suggests the prominence of institutional forces in shaping the wage equation, it should be possible to alter the shape by acting on these forces. In contrast to the view sometimes held, the present results specifically reject the notion that the wage equation has remained unchanged through time. Significantly different estimates of the equation were obtained for part of the 1920's and the postwar years, and a further change was noticeable in the postwar years after 1953.

The increased prominence of labor unions is the most obvious institutional change that occurred between the 1920's and the postwar period. Although no attempt was made to investigate the impact of the union movement directly, it seems likely that this was a major element in changing the wage relation between the two periods. The more inflationary nature of the wage relation for the postwar period is the most obvious aspect of the change. This is evident both in using explanatory data for the 1920's in the postwar equation, a procedure which generally overestimates the true wage changes that occurred, and in comparing the trend rate of wage increase for the 1920's with the trend rate of productivity increase for the period. If solely concerned with inflation, one then might want to attack the present strength of labor unions. But if the unions bear the major responsibility for the more inflationary current wage relation, they should also be credited with the greater stability of wage changes observed in the postwar economy. Nowhere in the postwar data do there appear the violent fluctuations of wages that were experienced in the early 1920's. Not only do present institutions keep wages from falling sharply under at least moderate recessions but they seem to prevent them from rising too rapidly when conditions arise that potentially are highly inflationary.

More important, labor unions are responsible for much more than an upward bias in the wage relation. They have been a pervasive influence in every aspect of labor's employer and community relations so that the single goal of over-all wage moderation offers insufficient warrant for making drastic changes in union structure even if it were possible to do so. Where specific questions regarding union power arise, careful study may suggest desirable changes. But the present findings are insufficient for this. They offer no evidence on the detailed workings of the bargaining process, the points at which power is exerted, or the particular circumstances under which the means at the disposal of a union may be excessive or insufficient to assure equity.

For similar reasons, the present estimate of the wage equation's structure offers no evidence in itself justifying an overhaul of industry's organization. For those industries that act with a degree of monopoly power in their product markets, a situation for which there are independent arguments for taking action, any steps taken that make profit rates competitive would aid the inflation problem as discussed earlier. But the wage equation itself offers insufficient basis for action on a broader scope than this. As with the questions of union power, this study says nothing of the workings of the pricing and bargaining processes that might suggest specific actions.

## Actions Within the Present Institutional Structure

If one accepts the present composition of wage-setting institutions, are there any policies that can alter the wage equation in a less inflationary direction? It would seem that there are possibilities in this direction. The British experience under the Labor Party after the war has been cited as an example of wage restraint in response to a reasoned appeal by the government. There seems to be skepticism about the potential of similar appeals in the United States; in fact, until recently they have never been seriously tried.

The appropriate role for the government in this area is hard to define, and a real danger exists that it may become overinvolved in the wage and price field. But against this possibility must be weighed the considerable advantages of successful steps for moderation.

One important task for the government is the education of labor, management, and the general public on the technical relation between wage changes, unit costs, productivity, and inflation. In its 1962 Annual Report,[2] the President's Council of Economic Advisers presented such an analysis in the form of guideposts for noninflationary wage and price behavior. It is perhaps a measure of how badly needed such an explanation was, and still is, that a considerable opposition to these guideposts immediately developed among those who believed they allocated *all* the gains of productivity increase to labor. Of course, they permit the returns to *all* inputs to increase at the same rate—depreciation, profits, interest, and fixed costs as well as wages.

In addition to its educational role in this area, the government can publicize the actions taken or contemplated by wage-deter-

[2] *Economic Report of the President, 1962* (Washington, D. C.: U.S. Government Printing Office, 1962).

mining groups and, where appropriate, by price-setting industries, measuring them against the guideposts. This is no abridgment of the principles of free collective bargaining and decentralized pricing; and it is the main resort open to the government for introducing the general interest in wage-price moderation into discretionary, private decisions.

While there is some risk of going too far, the possibility that at least some degree of improvement may be forthcoming from such policies of persuasion would seem to warrant the risk. The chances of shifting the inflation-unemployment relation by simple appeals from the government for moderation do not seem promising. On the other hand, the weight of the federal government could prove considerable if it is used to document and emphasize desirable standards and to arouse a public interest in measuring private decisions against these standards.

## A Final Assessment

In the absence of any such attempts to influence the economy's inflationary bent or, as seems likely, if such policies have a limited effectiveness, the possibilities for combining low unemployment with no inflation are not promising for the near future. There are some transitory conditions on the plus side, such as the recent history of price stability. But there are also possible minuses such as the corporate tax-rate reduction in the Revenue Act of 1964.

This means that zero inflation is an unrealistic target at least for the near future unless we are prepared to tolerate a continually slack economy to achieve it. But the degree of inflation that would be needed at present to bring the wage-productivity-price relation to equilibrium should be no more than about 2½ percent a year with a constant 4 percent unemployment rate. If there is some validity to the view that our price statistics are biased upward because they fail to account fully for quality improvements, the real inflation would be somewhat less. And if lower prices for imports and agricultural products could be achieved immediately, and if government persuasion for wage and price restraint were employed with some effectiveness, even this might be improved upon. In any case, the response of wages to price increases has been accounted for in this estimate, and it does not appear to lead to an explosive spiral. Thus, permitting a mild inflation should not invite an acceleration of price increases that would be intolerable.

Over a longer period, steps that would lower the profit rate-unemployment relation by desirable increases in competition and an increase of the equity base and capital stock are desirable and should prove effective. Tax measures that reduce profit rates could serve the single goal of restraining wage increases, but they must be viewed critically because of the likely reduction in investment incentives they would entail.

But major importance should be attached to maintaining low unemployment rates and minimizing cyclical variations. A number of reasons have been given here for expecting policies aimed at these ends to improve the inflation-unemployment relation as well. These included avoiding the unsymmetrical impact on wage changes of alternately high and low unemployment rates; minimizing the possibility of a ratchet effect in pricing that would arise from downward price rigidities; reducing the riskiness of investment so that lower expected profit rates would be acceptable for any given investment project; and finally, causing low unemployment to be associated with the average profit rates that must prevail over a period of time rather than the exceptional profit rates that prevail at cyclical peaks.

Without a careful analysis of the balance-of-payments situation and its prospects over the next few years, a final judgment cannot be made about how much inflation is tolerable. However, a few general observations can be advanced.

The relative prices of output traded internationally should continue to move favorably for the United States during the remainder of the 1960's. Even with wage increases that moderately exceed aggregate productivity gains, U.S. export prices need not rise. Exported goods are largely produced by industries that have had above average productivity growth in the past compared to the national average, and this situation is likely to continue. The sector typically cited for lowering the national average is the service sector, and its output is largely excluded from international trade. Some inflation generally may therefore mean no inflation of export prices. On the other hand, wages in most other industrialized countries have been rising more sharply since the wage-restraint policies that followed the war lost their urgency. A continuation of these trends should permit some upward drift in U.S. prices without intolerable consequences for its balance of trade. The income effect on imports of a more buoyant domestic economy would be adverse. But this could be at least partly offset as full employment diverted funds into domestic investment that would otherwise have gone abroad. Finally, the initial experience with voluntary restrictions on capital outflows and the possibility of using other specific steps to counter balance-of-payments problems add to the conclusion that the gold outflows of recent years need not interfere with a full-employment policy.

Yet, the redistributive aspects of inflation are another matter, and measures to correct for its worst consequences among the fixed income part of the population should be pursued. Improved retirement and welfare benefits and increased exemption levels for tax purposes are the kinds of measures that would be useful here. But this whole problem may be exaggerated in comparison with the redistributive aspects of high unemployment, at least for moderate rates of inflation.

Finally, if as has been argued here, the maintenance of high employment rates is one important way of improving the inflation-unemployment trade-off in the longer run, the case for pursuing full-employment policies becomes more urgent. If high unemployment were tolerated for a sufficiently long period, it seems likely that the economy would become "tight" at a high unemployment rate: deteriorating skills and increased immobility would become a problem for a larger fraction of the work force; profit rates would adjust to a normal level at the higher unemployment rate; and finally, optimal operating rates for existing industrial capacity would be reached while unemployment remained high. None of these would be irreversible, as our experience with war mobilization has shown. But reaching high employment rates would be more costly the longer we avoided it. In the longer run then, and within limits, the *tendency* at least may be for a given rate of inflation to exist with whatever unemployment rate we permit to become "normal." And to the extent this is so, it is a phenomenon that should be used to advantage rather than allowed to make our choices increasingly difficult.

# Appendix

### Part 1. A Description of the Sources of Data and Construction of Variables as They Are Used in the Study

*Wages*

The basic wage-rate statistic used is straight-time average hourly earnings of production workers, not adjusted for interindustry shifts. Series for all manufacturing and for the durable-goods and nondurable-goods subdivisions of manufacturing were taken from issues of the *Monthly Labor Review* starting in 1946. Nonwage benefits were not included in this wage variable, mainly because a satisfactory quarterly series was not available. Some experimenting with annual data including supplements suggested the results would not be affected seriously by this omission. The raw data were used to compute annual percentage changes for all manufacturing, and for the durable-goods and nondurable-goods subsectors. These variables are designed $w$, $^d w$, and $^n w$ respectively.

*Unemployment*

Three different measures of unemployment were collected. The first measures total unemployment as a percentage of the civilian labor force and was taken from the April 1960 issue of the *Survey of Current Business* and later issues of the same publication. This series was collected quarterly from 1947 to the present. The other two measures were for estimated unemployment rates in durable-goods and nondurable-goods industries. These were taken from worksheets supplied by the Bureau of Labor Statistics for the years 1949 through 1957; from the *Annual Report of the Labor Force* for 1958; and from *Employment and Earnings* for 1959 and 1960. The series were not available prior to 1949. In order to make the cover-

126

age comparable to that of the other data used, the years 1947 and 1948 were estimated from employment statistics in durable- and nondurable-goods industries and the civilian labor force unemployment figures for those years. From 1957 on, new definitions were used in the durable- and nondurable-goods unemployment series. The data following the definition change were multiplied by 0.9 to make them comparable with previous years.

The new raw data for each series were combined into four-quarter averages which constitute the basic unemployment variables for this study. These variables are designated $U$, $^dU$, and $^nU$, corresponding to the total civilian labor force and durable-goods and nondurable-goods series respectively.

### Cost of Living

The series used for the cost of living is the Consumer Price Index taken from issues of the *Monthly Labor Review*. It is an index with base 1947 to 1949 equal to 100. The forms of the variables constructed from the raw series are described in the text. They are designated $c$ and $c^*$.

### Profit Rate

Profit rate was measured as net profits after taxes as a percentage of stockholders' equity. The raw quarterly data for all manufacturing and for durable-goods and nondurable-goods were taken from issues of the Securities and Exchange Commission–Federal Trade Commission *Quarterly Financial Reports for U.S. Manufacturing Corporations*. For all three series, there were two times in the years covered when changes were made in the sampling procedure used which made it necessary to splice the data to obtain one continuous series for the whole period. The splicing was done on the assumption that the new benchmark year was correct and the error in the old series had increased linearly from its start. The variables used in the study were formed by taking four-quarter avarages of the profit-rate data. The resultant variables are designated, $R$, $^dR$, and $^nR$ for the three categories.

### Change in Profit Rate

A series for the change in profit rate was computed by taking first differences of the final profit-rate series described previously. These variables are designated $\Delta R$, $^d\Delta R$, and $^n\Delta R$.

### Output Prices

Output prices for the manufacturing sector were taken from *Wholesale Prices and Price Indexes, 1957,* and for later years from issues of the *Monthly Labor Review.* The index is based on 1947 to 1949 equal to 100. For use in testing, annual percentage changes of the index were calculated. The variable is indicated by $^m p$.

### Price of Services to Consumers

The index of the price of services to consumers was taken from *Bulletin Number 1256* of the Bureau of Labor Statistics for the years through 1958. Later years were taken from the *Monthly Labor Review.* The index is based on 1947 to 1949 equal to 100. Annual percentage changes of the data were calculated. The variable is labeled $^s p$.

### Crude Food Prices to Consumers

The information for this series is identical to that of the previous series, price of services to consumers. The variable is labeled $^f p$.

### Prices of Crude Nonfood Materials, except Fuel, for Manufacturing

This series was taken from *Economic Sector Indexes* for the years 1947 through 1954, and from *Bulletin Number 1214* for 1955 and 1956. Both publications are by the Bureau of Labor Statistics. For later years, the series was taken from the *Monthly Labor Review.* The series is based on 1947 to 1949 equal to 100. Annual percentage changes were computed for this study. The variable is indicated by $^r p$.

### Real Output

The Index of Manufacturing Production of the Federal Reserve Board was used to measure the real output of the manufacturing sector. The data were obtained from issues of the *Federal Reserve Bulletin.* There were two periods, in 1952 and 1958, when a new series was introduced. The ratio of the new series to the old during the period of overlap was used to splice the two. The resulting series has 1947 = 100. It is used with the series on capital stock, described next, to get a measure of the ratio of output to capacity.

### Manufacturing Capacity

The Index of Real Net Value of Manufacturing Structures and Equipment, computed by the Department of Commerce, was used to measure manufacturing capacity. The index has 1947 equal to 100. The data up to 1958 were taken from *U.S. Income and Output,* published in 1959 by the Department of Commerce. For later years, data were taken from issues of the *Survey of Current Business.* Only year-end figures were given, and quarterly data were constructed by linear interpolation within years. This series was used together with that for real output to get a measure of the ratio of output to capacity.

*Capacity Utilization*

The two preceding series for real output and capacity in manu-facturing were divided to give an index of capacity utilization. A four-quarter average of this index was then computed for use in the study. The variable is labeled $Q/K$.

*Change in Capacity Utilization*

The first difference of the final series of capacity utilization just described was computed to give a measure of the change in that series. The variable is labeled $\Delta(Q/K)$.

**Part 2. Variables for Period Spanned by the Regressions**

| Year | Qtr | $w$ | $d_w$ | $m_w$ |
|------|-----|------|------|------|
| 1948 | 1 | +10.43 | +10.08 | +11.01 |
| 1948 | 2 | +08.40 | +08.94 | +08.93 |
| 1948 | 3 | +09.02 | +09.37 | +09.57 |
| 1948 | 4 | +08.87 | +09.23 | +09.40 |
| 1949 | 1 | +07.87 | +09.16 | +06.61 |
| 1949 | 2 | +06.20 | +07.46 | +05.74 |
| 1949 | 3 | +03.01 | +02.86 | +02.38 |
| 1949 | 4 | +00.74 | +00.74 | +00.78 |
| 1950 | 1 | +00.73 | +00.70 | +01.55 |
| 1950 | 2 | +02.19 | +01.39 | +02.33 |
| 1950 | 3 | +03.65 | +02.78 | +03.10 |
| 1950 | 4 | +07.35 | +06.29 | +06.20 |
| 1951 | 1 | +08.70 | +08.33 | +07.63 |
| 1951 | 2 | +08.57 | +08.90 | +08.33 |
| 1951 | 3 | +08.45 | +09.46 | +08.27 |
| 1951 | 4 | +06.85 | +07.90 | +06.57 |
| 1952 | 1 | +05.33 | +05.77 | +04.96 |
| 1952 | 2 | +05.26 | +05.66 | +04.20 |
| 1952 | 3 | +04.55 | +04.93 | +03.47 |
| 1952 | 4 | +05.13 | +06.09 | +03.42 |
| 1953 | 1 | +06.33 | +07.27 | +04.05 |
| 1953 | 2 | +06.25 | +06.54 | +04.03 |
| 1953 | 3 | +06.83 | +07.06 | +05.37 |

PART 2 (*Continued*)

| *Year* | *Qtr* | *w* | *$d_w$* | *$m_w$* |
|------|-----|-----|-----|-----|
| 1953 | 4 | +06.10 | +05.17 | +05.30 |
| 1954 | 1 | +04.17 | +04.52 | +04.55 |
| 1954 | 2 | +03.53 | +03.91 | +04.52 |
| 1954 | 3 | +01.74 | +02.20 | +02.55 |
| 1954 | 4 | +01.72 | +02.73 | +01.89 |
| 1955 | 1 | +01.71 | +02.16 | +01.24 |
| 1955 | 2 | +02.27 | +02.69 | +01.85 |
| 1955 | 3 | +04.57 | +04.83 | +03.11 |
| 1955 | 4 | +04.52 | +04.79 | +03.70 |
| 1956 | 1 | +05.06 | +04.76 | +04.91 |
| 1956 | 2 | +05.56 | +05.23 | +06.06 |
| 1956 | 3 | +04.37 | +04.10 | +06.02 |
| 1956 | 4 | +05.95 | +05.58 | +05.95 |
| 1957 | 1 | +06.42 | +06.57 | +05.85 |
| 1957 | 2 | +05.26 | +05.47 | +04.57 |
| 1957 | 3 | +05.24 | +05.92 | +03.98 |
| 1957 | 4 | +04.08 | +04.81 | +03.93 |
| 1958 | 1 | +03.52 | +04.26 | +03.87 |
| 1958 | 2 | +03.50 | +04.24 | +03.28 |
| 1958 | 3 | +03.48 | +03.72 | +03.28 |
| 1958 | 4 | +02.94 | +03.67 | +02.70 |
| 1959 | 1 | +03.88 | +04.54 | +02.13 |
| 1959 | 2 | +04.35 | +04.98 | +02.65 |
| 1959 | 3 | +02.88 | +02.69 | +02.65 |
| 1959 | 4 | +03.33 | +02.21 | +03.16 |
| 1960 | 1 | +03.24 | +03.04 | +03.65 |
| 1960 | 2 | +02.78 | +02.59 | +03.61 |
| 1960 | 3 | +03.74 | +03.93 | +04.12 |

| *Year* | *Qtr* | *U* | *U*−1 | $d_U$−1 | $n_U$−1 |
|------|-----|-----|-----|-----|-----|
| 1948 | 2 | +3.825 | .2614 | .2703 | .2353 |
| 1948 | 3 | +3.725 | .2685 | .2778 | .2454 |
| 1948 | 4 | +3.800 | .2632 | .2667 | .2367 |
| 1949 | 1 | +4.025 | .2484 | .2260 | .2162 |
| 1949 | 2 | +4.550 | .2198 | .1869 | .1905 |
| 1949 | 3 | +5.250 | .1905 | .1521 | .1619 |
| 1949 | 4 | +6.050 | .1643 | .1347 | .1455 |
| 1950 | 1 | +6.475 | .1544 | .1270 | .1333 |
| 1950 | 2 | +6.425 | .1556 | .1342 | .1351 |
| 1950 | 3 | +5.950 | .1681 | .1575 | .1481 |
| 1950 | 4 | +5.250 | .1905 | .1887 | .1646 |
| 1951 | 1 | +4.525 | .2210 | .2500 | .1961 |
| 1951 | 2 | +3.900 | .2564 | .3175 | .2286 |
| 1951 | 3 | +3.550 | .2817 | .3704 | .2516 |
| 1951 | 4 | +3.350 | .2985 | .3883 | .2469 |
| 1952 | 1 | +3.250 | .3077 | .3883 | .2469 |

PART 2 (*Continued*)

| Year | Qtr | U | U−1 | dU−1 | nU−1 |
|------|-----|------|------|------|------|
| 1952 | 2 | +3.225 | .3101 | .3846 | .2564 |
| 1952 | 3 | +3.225 | .3101 | .3738 | .2649 |
| 1952 | 4 | +3.075 | .3252 | .4082 | .2985 |
| 1953 | 1 | +2.975 | .3361 | .4348 | .3200 |
| 1953 | 2 | +2.875 | .3478 | .4819 | .3419 |
| 1953 | 3 | +2.725 | .3670 | .5634 | .3540 |
| 1953 | 4 | +2.950 | .3390 | .4762 | .3390 |
| 1954 | 1 | +3.575 | .2797 | .3200 | .2778 |
| 1954 | 2 | +4.325 | .2312 | .2222 | .2186 |
| 1954 | 3 | +5.150 | .1942 | .1732 | .1877 |
| 1954 | 4 | +5.575 | .1794 | .1550 | .1754 |
| 1955 | 1 | +5.475 | .1827 | .1606 | .1754 |
| 1955 | 2 | +5.150 | .1942 | .1818 | .1932 |
| 1955 | 3 | +4.700 | .2128 | .2139 | .2162 |
| 1955 | 4 | +4.425 | .2260 | .2500 | .2247 |
| 1956 | 1 | +4.250 | .2353 | .2703 | .2424 |
| 1956 | 2 | +4.225 | .2367 | .2632 | .2353 |
| 1956 | 3 | +4.225 | .2367 | .2532 | .2235 |
| 1956 | 4 | +4.200 | .2381 | .2516 | .2260 |
| 1957 | 1 | +4.175 | .2395 | .2564 | .2247 |
| 1957 | 2 | +4.125 | .2424 | .2685 | .2210 |
| 1957 | 3 | +4.150 | .2410 | .2649 | .2186 |
| 1957 | 4 | +4.375 | .2286 | .2247 | .2107 |
| 1958 | 1 | +4.975 | .2010 | .1688 | .1887 |
| 1958 | 2 | +5.725 | .1747 | .1311 | .1667 |
| 1958 | 3 | +6.475 | .1544 | .1105 | .1521 |
| 1958 | 4 | +6.850 | .1460 | .1061 | .1465 |
| 1959 | 1 | +6.725 | .1487 | .1140 | .1509 |
| 1959 | 2 | +6.200 | .1613 | .1384 | .1681 |
| 1959 | 3 | +5.725 | .1747 | .1695 | .1843 |
| 1959 | 4 | +5.525 | .1810 | .1802 | .1896 |
| 1960 | 1 | +5.325 | .1878 | .2000 | .1923 |
| 1960 | 2 | +5.350 | .1869 | .1932 | .1942 |
| 1960 | 3 | +5.350 | .1869 | .1818 | .1923 |

| Year | Qtr | R | dR | nR | ΔR | dΔR | nΔR |
|------|-----|---------|---------|---------|--------|--------|--------|
| 1948 | 2 | +15.625 | +14.625 | +16.850 | +0.075 | +0.200 | +0.250 |
| 1948 | 3 | +15.900 | +15.375 | +16.975 | +0.275 | +0.750 | +0.125 |
| 1948 | 4 | +16.000 | +16.250 | +16.650 | +0.100 | +0.875 | −0.325 |
| 1949 | 1 | +14.975 | +15.775 | +15.075 | −1.025 | −0.47  | −1.575 |
| 1949 | 2 | +13.550 | +14.625 | +13.375 | −1.425 | −1.150 | −1.700 |
| 1949 | 3 | +12.525 | +13.700 | +12.175 | −1.025 | −0.925 | −1.200 |
| 1949 | 4 | +11.500 | +12.300 | +11.325 | −1.025 | −1.400 | −0.850 |
| 1950 | 1 | +11.300 | +12.100 | +11.100 | −0.200 | −0.200 | −0.225 |
| 1950 | 2 | +12.575 | +13.950 | +11.875 | +1.275 | +1.850 | +0.775 |
| 1950 | 3 | +13.950 | +15.650 | +13.800 | +1.375 | +1.700 | +1.175 |

PART 2 (*Continued*)

| Year | Qtr | $R$ | $^dR$ | $^nR$ | $\Delta R$ | $^d\Delta R$ | $^n\Delta R$ |
|------|-----|-----|-------|-------|------------|--------------|--------------|
| 1950 | 4 | +15.125 | +17.025 | +14.150 | +1.175 | +1.375 | +1.100 |
| 1951 | 1 | +15.750 | +17.800 | +14.950 | +0.625 | +0.775 | +0.800 |
| 1951 | 2 | +15.250 | +16.975 | +14.950 | −0.500 | −0.825 | +0.000 |
| 1951 | 3 | +13.425 | +14.725 | +13.650 | −1.825 | −2.250 | −1.300 |
| 1951 | 4 | +12.125 | +13.500 | +12.350 | −1.300 | −1.225 | −1.300 |
| 1952 | 1 | +11.075 | +12.175 | +11.100 | −1.050 | −1.325 | −1.250 |
| 1952 | 2 | +10.250 | +11.075 | +10.150 | −0.825 | −1.100 | −0.950 |
| 1952 | 3 | +10.225 | +11.025 | +09.850 | −0.025 | −0.050 | −0.300 |
| 1952 | 4 | +10.350 | +11.075 | +09.725 | +0.125 | +0.050 | −0.125 |
| 1953 | 1 | +10.525 | +11.275 | +09.875 | +0.175 | +0.200 | +0.150 |
| 1953 | 2 | +10.850 | +11.575 | +10.200 | +0.325 | +0.300 | +0.325 |
| 1953 | 3 | +11.025 | +11.900 | +10.250 | +0.175 | +0.325 | +0.050 |
| 1953 | 4 | +10.575 | +11.200 | +10.075 | −0.450 | −0.700 | −0.175 |
| 1954 | 1 | +10.250 | +10.675 | +09.950 | −0.325 | −0.525 | −0.125 |
| 1954 | 2 | +10.050 | +10.450 | +09.775 | −0.200 | −0.225 | −0.175 |
| 1954 | 3 | +09.750 | +10.000 | +09.625 | −0.300 | −0.450 | −0.150 |
| 1954 | 4 | +10.025 | +10.325 | +09.900 | +0.275 | +0.325 | +0.275 |
| 1955 | 1 | +10.525 | +11.100 | +10.200 | +0.500 | +0.775 | +0.300 |
| 1955 | 2 | +11.200 | +12.125 | +10.550 | +0.675 | +1.025 | +0.350 |
| 1955 | 3 | +11.975 | +13.025 | +11.175 | +0.775 | +0.900 | +0.625 |
| 1955 | 4 | +12.725 | +13.925 | +11.725 | +0.750 | +0.900 | +0.550 |
| 1956 | 1 | +12.975 | +14.050 | +11.975 | +0.250 | +0.125 | +0.250 |
| 1956 | 2 | +12.925 | +13.750 | +12.125 | −0.050 | −0.300 | +0.150 |
| 1956 | 3 | +12.550 | +13.125 | +11.975 | −0.375 | −0.625 | −0.150 |
| 1956 | 4 | +12.275 | +12.775 | +11.775 | −0.275 | −0.350 | −0.200 |
| 1957 | 1 | +12.125 | +12.625 | +11.675 | −0.150 | −0.150 | −0.100 |
| 1957 | 2 | +11.775 | +12.275 | +11.325 | −0.350 | −0.350 | −0.350 |
| 1957 | 3 | +11.650 | +12.225 | +11.125 | −0.125 | −0.050 | −0.200 |
| 1957 | 4 | +10.950 | +11.300 | +10.625 | −0.700 | −0.925 | −0.500 |
| 1958 | 1 | +09.675 | +09.150 | +09.725 | −1.275 | −1.650 | −0.900 |
| 1958 | 2 | +08.725 | +08.300 | +09.150 | −0.950 | −1.350 | −0.575 |
| 1958 | 3 | +08.350 | +07.650 | +09.025 | −0.375 | −0.650 | −0.125 |
| 1958 | 4 | +08.575 | +07.975 | +09.175 | +0.225 | +0.325 | +0.150 |
| 1959 | 1 | +09.375 | +09.000 | +09.725 | +0.800 | +1.025 | +0.550 |
| 1959 | 2 | +10.550 | +10.700 | +10.400 | +1.175 | +1.700 | +0.675 |
| 1959 | 3 | +10.700 | +10.825 | +10.600 | +0.150 | +0.125 | +0.200 |
| 1959 | 4 | +10.425 | +10.375 | +10.450 | −0.275 | −0.450 | −0.150 |
| 1960 | 1 | +10.375 | +10.325 | +10.400 | −0.050 | −0.050 | −0.050 |
| 1960 | 2 | +09.725 | +09.350 | +10.100 | −0.650 | −0.975 | −0.300 |
| 1960 | 3 | +09.500 | +09.050 | +09.925 | −0.225 | −0.300 | −0.175 |

| Year | Qtr | $c$ | $^mp$ | $^rp$ | $^fp$ | $^sp$ |
|------|-----|-----|-------|-------|-------|-------|
| 1948 | 2 | +8.776 | +08.995 | +1.486 | +0.876 | +06.75 |
| 1948 | 3 | +8.146 | +09.242 | +1.232 | +0.862 | +06.47 |
| 1948 | 4 | +4.996 | +05.015 | +0.551 | +0.401 | +06.06 |
| 1949 | 1 | +1.433 | +00.391 | −0.057 | −0.454 | +05.79 |

PART 2 (*Continued*)

| Year | Qtr | $c$ | $^mp$ | $^rp$ | $^fp$ | $^sp$ |
|------|-----|-----|-------|-------|-------|-------|
| 1949 | 2 | −0.254 | −02.718 | −1.201 | −0.337 | +05.12 |
| 1949 | 3 | −2.796 | −05.608 | −1.338 | −0.213 | +03.63 |
| 1949 | 4 | −2.135 | −05.444 | −1.166 | −1.109 | +03.49 |
| 1950 | 1 | −1.476 | −03.119 | −0.709 | −1.478 | +03.07 |
| 1950 | 2 | −0.682 | −00.299 | +0.746 | −1.670 | +02.96 |
| 1950 | 3 | +1.981 | +06.445 | +2.446 | −1.048 | +03.31 |
| 1950 | 4 | +4.301 | +11.717 | +3.675 | +0.698 | +03.75 |
| 1951 | 1 | +8.682 | +17.103 | +4.443 | +1.401 | +05.31 |
| 1951 | 2 | +8.990 | +15.721 | +3.236 | +1.945 | +05.38 |
| 1951 | 3 | +6.982 | +08.704 | +0.371 | +1.481 | +05.31 |
| 1951 | 4 | +6.397 | +03.436 | −0.842 | +1.156 | +05.14 |
| 1952 | 1 | +2.716 | −02.319 | −1.756 | +0.813 | +03.98 |
| 1952 | 2 | +2.156 | −03.009 | −1.773 | +0.519 | +04.93 |
| 1952 | 3 | +2.768 | −01.654 | −0.923 | +1.232 | +04.61 |
| 1952 | 4 | +1.328 | −01.923 | −0.970 | +0.089 | +04.64 |
| 1953 | 1 | +0.892 | −01.495 | −0.779 | −0.183 | +04.34 |
| 1953 | 2 | +0.888 | −00.355 | −0.476 | −0.294 | +03.77 |
| 1953 | 3 | +0.704 | +00.531 | −0.183 | −1.123 | +04.24 |
| 1953 | 4 | +0.791 | +00.980 | −0.355 | −0.992 | +03.53 |
| 1954 | 1 | +1.229 | +01.518 | −0.488 | −0.991 | +03.34 |
| 1954 | 2 | +0.702 | +01.335 | −0.217 | −1.399 | +02.83 |
| 1954 | 3 | +0.000 | +00.176 | −0.308 | −0.685 | +02.15 |
| 1954 | 4 | −0.522 | +00.088 | +0.184 | −0.955 | +01.82 |
| 1955 | 1 | −0.260 | +00.088 | +0.573 | +0.261 | +01.74 |
| 1955 | 2 | −0.173 | +00.176 | +0.299 | +0.819 | +01.81 |
| 1955 | 3 | +0.090 | +01.494 | +0.760 | +0.093 | +01.81 |
| 1955 | 4 | +0.699 | +02.734 | +0.722 | +0.647 | +01.89 |
| 1956 | 1 | +0.263 | +03.251 | +0.756 | +0.223 | +01.71 |
| 1956 | 2 | +1.048 | +04.382 | +0.645 | +0.168 | +02.08 |
| 1956 | 3 | +1.997 | +03.810 | +0.009 | −0.164 | +02.45 |
| 1956 | 4 | +2.507 | +04.206 | +0.080 | −0.273 | +02.67 |
| 1957 | 1 | +3.447 | +04.160 | −0.139 | −0.789 | +03.89 |
| 1957 | 2 | +3.589 | +03.191 | −0.167 | −0.776 | +03.93 |
| 1957 | 3 | +3.376 | +03.169 | +0.125 | +0.073 | +03.89 |
| 1957 | 4 | +3.023 | +01.977 | −0.580 | +0.968 | +04.17 |
| 1958 | 1 | +3.415 | +01.387 | −0.687 | +2.244 | +03.96 |
| 1958 | 2 | +3.221 | +01.302 | −0.652 | +1.277 | +03.49 |
| 1958 | 3 | +2.297 | +00.728 | −0.530 | +0.031 | +03.03 |
| 1958 | 4 | +1.966 | +00.808 | +0.215 | −0.702 | +02.50 |
| 1959 | 1 | +0.814 | +00.805 | +0.397 | −1.409 | +01.91 |
| 1959 | 2 | +0.404 | +01.044 | +0.641 | −1.174 | +02.18 |
| 1959 | 3 | +0.967 | +00.883 | +0.345 | −0.486 | +02.73 |
| 1959 | 4 | +1.367 | +00.401 | +0.119 | −0.469 | +03.00 |
| 1960 | 1 | +1.528 | +00.399 | −0.127 | −0.064 | +03.32 |
| 1960 | 2 | +1.762 | +00.079 | −0.404 | +0.970 | +02.96 |
| 1960 | 3 | +1.354 | +00.000 | −0.586 | +0.532 | +02.65 |

PART 2 (*Continued*)

| Year | Qtr | Q/K | Δ(Q/K) | Year | Qtr | Q/K | Δ(Q/K) |
|------|-----|------|--------|------|-----|------|--------|
| 1948 | 2 | 098.0 | −0.6 | 1954 | 3 | 093.6 | −2.5 |
| 1948 | 3 | 097.3 | −0.7 | 1954 | 4 | 093.8 | +0.2 |
| 1948 | 4 | 096.0 | −1.3 | 1955 | 1 | 095.5 | +1.7 |
| 1949 | 1 | 094.2 | −1.8 | 1955 | 2 | 097.9 | +2.4 |
| 1949 | 2 | 090.6 | −3.6 | 1955 | 3 | 100.5 | +2.6 |
| 1949 | 3 | 088.2 | −2.4 | 1955 | 4 | 102.5 | +2.0 |
| 1949 | 4 | 086.4 | −1.8 | 1956 | 1 | 102.6 | +0.1 |
| 1950 | 1 | 086.0 | −0.4 | 1956 | 2 | 102.0 | −0.6 |
| 1950 | 2 | 089.3 | +3.3 | 1956 | 3 | 101.6 | −0.4 |
| 1950 | 3 | 092.9 | +3.6 | 1956 | 4 | 101.0 | −0.6 |
| 1950 | 4 | 097.0 | +4.1 | 1957 | 1 | 100.6 | −0.4 |
| 1951 | 1 | 100.9 | +3.9 | 1957 | 2 | 100.3 | −0.3 |
| 1951 | 2 | 102.7 | +1.8 | 1957 | 3 | 099.3 | −1.0 |
| 1951 | 3 | 102.7 | +0.0 | 1957 | 4 | 096.5 | −2.8 |
| 1951 | 4 | 101.7 | −1.0 | 1958 | 1 | 092.8 | −3.7 |
| 1952 | 1 | 100.4 | −1.3 | 1958 | 2 | 090.1 | −2.7 |
| 1952 | 2 | 097.7 | −2.7 | 1958 | 3 | 088.6 | −1.5 |
| 1952 | 3 | 097.8 | +0.1 | 1958 | 4 | 089.1 | +0.5 |
| 1952 | 4 | 098.8 | +1.0 | 1959 | 1 | 092.4 | +3.3 |
| 1953 | 1 | 101.0 | +2.2 | 1959 | 2 | 096.5 | +4.1 |
| 1953 | 2 | 104.2 | +3.2 | 1959 | 3 | 097.9 | +1.4 |
| 1953 | 3 | 104.4 | +0.2 | 1959 | 4 | 099.9 | +2.0 |
| 1953 | 4 | 102.2 | −2.2 | 1960 | 1 | 100.8 | +0.9 |
| 1954 | 1 | 099.2 | −3.0 | 1960 | 2 | 100.3 | −0.5 |
| 1954 | 2 | 096.1 | −3.1 | 1960 | 3 | 100.0 | −0.3 |

## Part 3. Variables for Period Beyond Years Spanned by the Regressions

| Year | Quarter | $w$ | $c$ | $R$ | $\Delta R$ | $U$ |
|------|---------|------|------|-------|--------|------|
| 1960 | 4 | 3.23 | 1.47 | 9.20 | −0.30 | 5.63 |
| 1961 | 1 | 2.28 | 1.46 | 8.45 | −0.75 | 6.03 |
| 1961 | 2 | 2.74 | 0.97 | 8.28 | −0.17 | 6.43 |
| 1961 | 3 | 2.74 | 1.06 | 8.30 | +0.02 | 6.73 |
| 1961 | 4 | 3.17 | 0.77 | 8.83 | +0.53 | 6.70 |
| 1962 | 1 | 2.68 | 0.87 | 9.38 | +0.45 | 6.43 |
| 1962 | 2 | 2.67 | 1.25 | 9.65 | +0.27 | 6.10 |
| 1962 | 3 | 2.22 | 1.25 | 9.78 | +0.13 | 5.78 |
| 1962 | 4 | 2.19 | 1.24 | 9.78 | 0.00 | 5.58 |
| 1963 | 1 | 2.17 | 1.24 | 9.68 | −0.10 | 5.60 |
| 1963 | 2 | 2.60 | 1.05 | 9.85 | +0.17 | 5.68 |
| 1963 | 3 | 3.04 | 1.32 | 10.03 | +0.18 | 5.65 |
| 1963 | 4 | 3.00 | 1.42 | 10.25 | +0.22 | 5.70 |

# Bibliography

**References**

Bhatia, Rattan J., "Profits and the Rate of Change in Money Earnings in the United States, 1935–1959," *Economica*, N.S. 29 (August 1962).

Bhatia, Rattan J., "Unemployment and the Rate of Change of Money Earnings in the United States, 1900–1958," *Economica*, N.S. 28 (August 1961).

Bowen, William G., *Wage Behavior in the Postwar Period–An Empirical Analysis* (Princeton, N.J.: Princeton University Press, 1960).

Bronfenbrenner, Martin, and Franklyn D. Holzman, "Survey of Inflation Theory," *American Economic Review*, Vol. LIII (September 1963).

Brown, A. J., *The Great Inflation, 1939–1951* (London: Oxford University Press, 1955).

Chow, Gregory C., "Tests of Equality Between Sets of Coefficients in Two Linear Regressions," *Econometrica*, Vol. 28 (July 1960).

Dicks-Mireaux, L. A., and J. C. R. Dow, "The Determinants of Wage Inflation: United Kingdom 1946–1956," *Journal of the Royal Statistical Society*, Series A, 22(2) (1959).

Dow, J. C. R., and L. A. Dicks-Mireaux, "The Excess Demand for Labor," *Oxford Economic Papers*, N.S. 10 (February 1958).

Duesenberry, James S., Otto Eckstein, and Gary Fromm, "A Simulation of the United States Economy in Recession," *Econometrica*, Vol. 28 (October 1960).

Eckstein, Otto, "A Theory of the Wage-Price Process in Modern Industry," *The Review of Economic Studies*, 31(4) (October 1964).

Eckstein, Otto, and Thomas A. Wilson, "The Determination of Money Wages in American Industry," *Quarterly Journal of Economics*, Vol. 72 (August 1962).

*Economic Report of the President, January 1962* (Washington, D. C.: U.S. Government Printing Office, 1962).

Epstein, Ralph C., *Industrial Profits in the United States* (New York: National Bureau of Economic Research, Inc., 1934).

135

Garbarino, Joseph W., "Unionism and the General Wage Level," *American Economic Review*, Vol. 40 (December 1950).

Haavelmo, Trygve, "Methods of Measuring the Marginal Propensity to Consume," Chapter IV in *Studies in Econometric Method*, Cowles Commission Monograph 14, W. C. Hood, T. C. Koopmans, ed. (New York: John Wiley & Sons, Inc., 1953).

Hines, A. G., "Trade Unions and Wage Inflation in the United Kingdom, 1893–1961," *The Review of Economic Studies*, 31(4) (October 1964)

Kalacheck, Edward, *The Determinants of Higher Unemployment Rates, 1958–1960*, unpublished doctoral dissertation, Massachusetts Institute of Technology, 1963.

Kaldor, Nicholas, "Economic Growth and the Problem of Inflation," *Economica*, N.S. 26 (November 1959).

Klein, L. R., and R. J. Ball, "Some Econometrics of the Determination of Absolute Prices and Wages," *Economic Journal*, Vol. 69 (September 1959).

Knowles, K. G. J. C., and C. B. Winsten, "Can the Level of Unemployment Explain Changes in Wages?" *Bulletin of the Oxford University Institute of Statistics*, Vol. 21 (1959).

Kuh, Edwin, "Profits, Profit Markups, and Productivity," Study Paper No. 15, Joint Economic Committee, Washington, D. C., 1960.

Lebergott, Stanley, "Annual Estimates of Unemployment in the United States, 1900–1954," *The Measurement and Behavior of Unemployment* (Princeton, N. J.: Princeton University Press, 1957).

Levinson, Harold M., "Postwar Movement of Prices and Wages in Manufacturing Industries," in *Study of Employment, Growth, and Price Levels*, Study Paper No. 21, Joint Economic Committee, Washington, D. C.: 1960.

Lipsey, Richard G., "The Relation Between Unemployment and the Rate of Change of Money Wage Rates in the United Kingdom 1862–1957: A Further Analysis," *Economica*, N.S. 27 (February 1960).

Lipsey, Richard, and M. D. Stever, "The Relation Between Profits and Wage Rates," *Economica*, Vol. 28 (May 1961).

Phillips, A. W., "The Relation Between Unemployment and the Rate of Change of Money Wage Rates in the United Kingdom, 1861–1957," *Economica*, N.S. 25 (November 1958).

President's Committee to Appraise Employment and Unemployment Statistics, *Measuring Employment and Unemployment* (Washington, D. C.: U.S. Government Printing Office, 1962).

Rees, Albert, "Patterns of Wages, Prices and Productivity," *Wages, Prices and Productivity*, The American Assembly, Columbia University, 1959.

Samuelson, Paul A., and Robert M. Solow, "Analytical Aspects of Anti-Inflation Policy," *Papers and Proceedings of the American Economic Association,* Vol. 50 (May 1960).

Schultze, Charles L., Study Paper No. 1, "Recent Inflation in the United States," Joint Economic Committee, Washington, D. C., September 1959.

Simler, Norman J., "Long-term Unemployment, the Structural Hypothesis, and Public Policy," *American Economic Review,* Vol. 54 (December 1964).

Theil, Henri, *Economic Forecasts and Policy* (Amsterdam: North Holland Publishing Co., 1958).

Theil, Henri, *The Linear Aggregation of Economic Relations* (Amsterdam: North Holland Publishing Co., 1954).

Woytinsky, W. S., *Labor and Management Look at Collective Bargaining* (New York: Twentieth Century Fund, 1949).

### Data Sources

Epstein, Ralph C., *Industrial Profits in the United States* (New York: National Bureau of Economic Research, Inc., 1934).

Lebergott, Stanley, "Annual Estimates of Unemployment in the United States, 1900–1954," *The Measurement and Behavior of Unemployment* (Princeton, N. J.: Princeton University Press, 1957).

Rees, Albert, "Patterns of Wages, Prices and Productivity," *Wages, Prices and Productivity,* The American Assembly, Columbia University, 1959.

Securities and Exchange Commission–Federal Trade Commission, *Quarterly Financial Reports for U.S. Manufacturing Corporations,* issues from 1947 through 1961.

U.S. Department of Commerce, *Survey of Current Business,* various issues.

U.S. Department of Commerce, *U.S. Income and Output,* Washington, D. C., 1958.

U.S. Department of Labor, various publications of the Bureau of Labor Statistics including  a. *Annual Report on the Labor Force,* 1958. b. *Economic Sector Indexes,* 1947–1954. c. *Employment and Earnings,* 1959 and 1960. d. *Monthly Labor Review,* 1950 through 1960. e. *Wholesale Prices and Price Indexes, 1957. f.* Bulletin No. 1214. g. Bulletin No. 1256.